# HIKING IN HONG KONG

## HONG KONG, LANTAU, MACLEHOSE AND WILSON TRAILS AND 21 DAY WALKS

by Andrew Mok and Simon Whitmarsh

JUNIPER HOUSE, MURLEY MOSS,
OXENHOLME ROAD, KENDAL, CUMBRIA LA9 7RL
www.cicerone.co.uk

© Andrew Mok and Simon Whitmarsh 2022
First edition 2022
ISBN: 978 1 78631 051 4

Printed in China on responsibly sourced paper on behalf of Latitude Press
A catalogue record for this book is available from the British Library.
All photographs are by the author unless otherwise stated.

Route mapping by Lovell Johns www.lovelljohns.com
Contains OpenStreetMap.org data © OpenStreetMap
contributors, CC-BY-SA. NASA relief data courtesy of ESRI

## Acknowledgements

Thank you to our parents Mr and Mrs YC Mok, and Paul and Elizabeth
Whitmarsh, for giving us opportunities and limitless support.

## Updates to this guide

While every effort is made by our authors to ensure the accuracy of guidebooks
as they go to print, changes can occur during the lifetime of an edition. This
guidebook was researched and written before and during the COVID-19 pan-
demic. While we are not aware of any significant changes to routes or facilities
at the time of printing, it is likely that the current situation will give rise to more
changes than would usually be expected. Any updates that we know of for this
guide will be on the Cicerone website (www.cicerone.co.uk/1051/updates), so
please check before planning your trip. We also advise that you check information about such things as transport, accommodation and shops locally. Even
rights of way can be altered over time.

We are always grateful for information about any discrepancies between
a guidebook and the facts on the ground, sent by email to updates@cicerone.
co.uk or by post to Cicerone, Juniper House, Murley Moss, Oxenholme Road,
Kendal, LA9 7RL.

**Register your book:** To sign up to receive free updates, special offers and
GPX files where available, register your book at www.cicerone.co.uk.

*Front cover:* Looking towards Lion Rock, the emblem representing the 'never
give up' spirit of the city

# CONTENTS

## Note on mapping

The route maps in this guide are derived from publicly available data, data-bases and crowd-sourced data. As such they have not been through the detailed checking procedures that would generally be applied to a published map from an official mapping agency. However, we have reviewed them closely in the light of local knowledge as part of the preparation of this guide.

# Symbols used on route maps

| | | | |
|---|---|---|---|
| route | | lighthouse |
| alternative route | | peak |
| start point | | campsite |
| finish point | | building |
| start/finish point | | viewpoint |
| alternative start/finish point | | bridge |
| alternative start point | | transmitter station |
| alternative finish point | | obelisk |
| route direction | | cave |
| woodland | | other feature |
| urban areas | | water feature |
| station/railway | | toilets |
| underground railway | | refreshments |
| motorway tunnel | | shelter |
| | | cable car route |

### Relief
in metres

| | |
|---|---|
| 800–1000 | |
| 600–800 | |
| 400–600 | |
| 200–400 | |
| 0–200 | |

SCALE: 1:50,000

Contour lines are drawn at 25m intervals and highlighted at 100m intervals.

**GPX files** for all routes can be downloaded free at www.cicerone.co.uk/1051/GPX.

# ROUTE SUMMARY TABLES

## Hong Kong Trail

| Stage | Distance | Ascent | Grade | Time | Page |
|-------|----------|--------|-------|------|------|
| Day 1 | 18km | 1400m | difficult | 5hr 45min | 34 |
| Day 2 | 16km | 980m | difficult | 5hr 30min | 40 |
| Day 3 | 16km | 1050m | difficult | 4hr 45min | 45 |
| **Total** | **50km** | **3430m** | | **16hr** | |

## Lantau Trail

| Stage | Distance | Ascent | Grade | Time | Page |
|-------|----------|--------|-------|------|------|
| Day 1 | 14.5km | 1560m | challenging | 6hr | 54 |
| Day 2 | 16km | 670m | difficult | 5hr 30min | 61 |
| Day 3 | 17.25km | 1020m | difficult | 6hr | 68 |
| Day 4 | 14km | 760m | moderate | 4hr | 72 |
| Day 5 | 12km | 540m | moderate | 4hr | 76 |
| **Total** | **73.75km** | **4550m** | | **25hr 30min** | |

## MacLehose Trail

| Stage | Distance | Ascent | Grade | Time | Page |
|-------|----------|--------|-------|------|------|
| Day 1 | 24.5km | 1340m | challenging | 8hr 30min | 88 |
| Day 2 | 10.25km | 670m | moderate | 3hr 45min | 94 |
| Day 3 | 23.5km | 1770m | challenging | 9hr | 98 |
| Day 4 | 20.75km | 1680m | challenging | 8hr 15min | 105 |
| Day 5 | 22.5km | 990m | difficult | 6hr 30min | 111 |
| **Total** | **101.5km** | **6450m** | | **36hr** | |

## Wilson Trail

| Stage | Distance | Ascent | Grade | Time | Page |
|-------|----------|--------|-------|------|------|
| Day 1 | 11.5km | 1040m | difficult | 5hr | 122 |
| Day 2 | 9.25km | 560m | moderate | 3hr 30min | 126 |
| Day 3 | 16km | 1270m | difficult | 6hr | 131 |
| Day 4 | 20.5km | 1080m | difficult | 6hr 45min | 136 |
| Day 5 | 23km | 1470m | challenging | 9hr | 143 |
| **Total** | **80.25km** | **5420m** | | **30hr 15min** | |

## Day walks

| Walk | | Distance | Ascent | Grade | Time | Page |
|---|---|---|---|---|---|---|
| Walk 1 | Big Knife Mountain | 8.75km | 560m | moderate | 3hr 30min | 154 |
| Walk 2 | Tai Lam Chung Reservoir Circuit | 22.5km | 1200m | difficult | 6hr 30min | 158 |
| Walk 3 | Yuen Tsuen Ancient Trail | 14.5km | 730m | moderate | 4hr 30min | 164 |
| Walk 4 | Ben Nevis | 8km | 600m | difficult | 4hr | 170 |
| Walk 5 | Tung Ping Chau | 7km | 140m | easy | 3hr | 175 |
| Walk 6 | Hanging Lantern and the ghost villages | 17km | 810m | difficult | 6hr 15min | 180 |
| Walk 7 | Wong Leng and Bride's Pool | 10.5km | 780m | difficult | 4hr 30min | 187 |
| Walk 8 | Plover Cove Reservoir Country Trail | 18.5km | 780m | difficult | 6hr 30min | 192 |
| Walk 9 | Tai Po Kau Nature Reserve | 10.5km | 660m | easy | 4hr | 197 |
| Walk 10 | Lion Rock and the walk of many hills | 11.75km | 1080m | challenging | 6hr | 200 |
| Walk 11 | Tai Tan and Cheung Sheung Country Trails | 16km | 800m | moderate | 5hr 30min | 206 |
| Walk 12 | Ma On Shan Country Park | 9.5km | 680m | moderate | 4hr | 212 |
| Walk 13 | Ko Lau Wan to Sharp Peak | 15.5km | 1080m | challenging | 7hr | 217 |
| Walk 14 | High Junk Peak | 8.75km | 600m | moderate | 3hr 30min | 223 |
| Walk 15 | Chi Ma Wan Country Trail (extended version) | 21.5km | 1250m | difficult | 7hr 15min | 227 |
| Walk 16 | Cheung Chau | 12.5km | 470m | moderate | 4hr 30min | 231 |
| Walk 17 | Violet Hill | 5.25km | 400m | easy | 2hr 15min | 235 |
| Walk 18 | Tung Lung Chau | 7.25km | 520m | easy | 3hr 30min | 240 |
| Walk 19 | Mount Stenhouse, Lamma Island | 9km | 620m | challenging | 4hr 30min | 244 |
| Walk 20 | From pier to pier, Lamma Island | 6.25km | 270m | easy | 2hr 15min | 249 |
| Walk 21 | Po Toi Island | 6.25km | 340m | easy | 2hr 30min | 253 |

Looking back at some of the many steps of Section 5 of Hong Kong Trail (Day 2)

# PREFACE

When we came together – one of us born in Hong Kong and the other a frequent visitor to the area – to write this guide, little did we know what wonderful hiking opportunities awaited us in the Pearl of the Orient. We could not have been more wrong in thinking that hiking here would be like an easy stroll or a city tour, and our eyes were opened to the hidden, nature-filled beauty of this former British colony. The highest mountain, Tai Mo Shan, is only 957m, nothing compared to Everest, but the steep peaks and hilly landscapes of the entire area definitely give a good cardiovascular workout.

Writing this book involved us in walking extensively around all parts of the territory: hiking up some of its top 100 highest peaks, including Hong Kong's own Ben Nevis, enjoying panoramic views, circumnavigating some of the 262 outlying islands, and relishing the challenge of completing all four long-distance trails – we were astounded at what it had to offer.

We thoroughly enjoyed doing the research for this book, discovering places that even a local such as Andrew had never seen. We hope that, with its insider tips and vignettes of local information, the book will bring you as much enjoyment.

*Andrew and Simon*

*Ma On Shan looms over the path (MacLehose Trail, Day 3)*

# INTRODUCTION

*Nearly at the top of Needle Hill (MacLehose Trail, Day 4)*

Hong Kong (香港 pronounced Heung Gong, meaning Fragrant Harbour) is simply 'home' to over 7.5 million locals. The name conjures up ideas of a vibrant city of multi-culturalism where East meets West, a foodie haven where it is possible to eat astoundingly well by day and night, an exciting shopping venue for almost anything and, most of all, a densely populated metropolis famous for its skyscraper landscape. It has the highest number of vertiginous buildings in the world, twice as many as New York, but if you think it is a complete concrete jungle, come hiking in Hong Kong and be very pleasantly surprised. The widely held idea of Hong Kong as an amazing skyline tells only a tiny part of the story, for it also provides the nature and challenges that serious hikers crave.

Hong Kong is 75 per cent countryside, with 440 square kilometres (40 per cent of the land mass) protected area. It is made up of a series of volcanic peaks, where the flat areas (natural or man-made) are developed, leaving steep hilly landscapes as conservation areas, offering fantastic ridge walks and superb panoramic views. The mountains are not massive but the steep ascents and descents provide great challenges; liking steps is an advantage!

*Hexagonal columns of Po Pin Chau (MacLehose Trail, Day 1)*

Within a relatively small geographical area, it is possible to climb mountains, walk through mangrove swamps, visit old fishing villages, see wild boar or pangolin, go tropical birdwatching, explore unique geological features, and admire the astounding numbers and varieties of butterflies. There are options to camp on remote beaches for stargazing, or to be whisked off to five-star hotels and eat in Michelin-starred restaurants, should your preference and budget be that way inclined. With the efficient transport system, it is surprisingly easy to leave the hustle and bustle of this international business centre behind, giving hikers easy access to nature.

Once stunning views, challenging climbs and massive multi-day hikes are added into the mix of gentler family-orientated strolls through national parks and nature reserves, the place becomes interesting to hikers of all grades looking for something a bit different. Hong Kong cannot be described as wilderness; it is for people who appreciate that the famous skyscraper landscape can add an extra dimension as a background to startling natural beauty. In addition, this is an archipelago of 263 islands nestling in the South China Sea, providing opportunities for circumnavigation of the islands as well as many coastal walks visiting white-sanded beaches.

Visit Hong Kong for an East-meets-West extravaganza? Yes! But why not add UNESCO-listed geology

(Walk 5, or Section 2 of MacLehose Trail); ridge walks high above the concrete jungle (Walk 10); or wildlife-watching, ranging from eagles to dolphins (Lantau Trail). Whether visiting for mere days or for longer, there are hikes here to astound, to challenge, to excite, to surprise, and, above all, to provide calming nature in contrast to the bustling, frenetic metropolis. Hiking is one of the locals' favourite pastimes, and Hong Kong has also become renowned worldwide as a hiking destination with award-winning walks such as the Dragon's Back and MacLehose Trail.

This book covers the length and breadth of this surprisingly diverse territory. It includes all four long-distance trails (Hong Kong, Lantau, MacLehose and Wilson), broken into chunks of reasonable size with emphasis on ease of access via public transport, and with camping information where relevant. The day walks range from easier hikes suitable for families or those with limited time, to challenging hikes up to fantastic summits including the top ten highest mountains, and trails in more remote areas.

## ABOUT HONG KONG

The official name is the Hong Kong Special Administrative Region of the People's Republic of China, abbreviated to SAR. It is both part of China and administratively separate under the 'one country, two systems' principle, which has been in place since Hong Kong ceased being a British protectorate in 1997.

Covering a total area of 2755 square kilometres, it consists of Hong Kong Island (the second largest island), Lantau Island (the biggest island), Kowloon Peninsula and the New Territories bordering mainland China, plus another 261 islands. It is surrounded by the South China Sea on three sides.

It is famous for its harbour views, skyscraper landscape, food (especially Cantonese cuisine), and film stars, including Bruce Lee; it remains an incredibly important centre for world trade and is one of the richest cities in the world. The population has increased from 3 million in the 1960s to 7.5 million.

There is a significant amount of greenery in Hong Kong. This is because building on steep slopes is difficult, so development tends to be on the flat of the shoreline or on reclaimed land, leaving the hills to nature. This is further helped by ample amounts of water, especially during the typhoon season, and most plants and trees are evergreen due to the subtropical climate.

Frequently encountered are catchwaters, channels for rainwater drainage, which are necessary for both protecting slopes (see MacLehose Trail, Section 10) and filling the many reservoirs of Hong Kong.

## GEOLOGY

Hong Kong is 85 per cent volcanic in origin, mostly igneous rock, including granite, which is slowly cooled magma. It only became the archipelago that it is today when the sea levels rose at the end of the last ice age.

The Hong Kong Global Geopark is UNESCO-listed and consists of two main areas. The best displays of its explosive volcanic past can be seen in the Sai Kung area, where the incredibly rare pink hexagonal columns are very similar in appearance to the Giant's Causeway in Ireland but with a different formation process. The columns are silica-rich volcanic rock as opposed to the dark grey basalt columns found elsewhere. Po Pin Chau (nicknamed Giant Pipe Organ) and the twisted hexagonal columns near East Dam are good examples (MacLehose Trail, Section 2).

The second geopark area is in the North East New Territories, showcasing the rarer sedimentary rocks. The best places to appreciate these are Tung Ping Chau (Walk 5) for multiple layers of the youngest, attractively eroded rocks, or Ma On Shan (Walk 12) and Plover Cove area (Walks 7 and 8) for the oldest Devonian ones.

## WILDLIFE

**Birds**

A staggering 530 bird species are found in Hong Kong. This is due to its subtropical climate and highly varied environments (coastal, shrublands, woodlands and wetlands), as well as its location on a major migratory

*The red-whiskered bulbul*

route, the East Asian–Australasian Flyway. Good walks for seeing birds are Lantau Trail, Tai Po Kau (Walk 9) and Po Toi Island (Walk 21).

Frequently encountered are red-whiskered bulbul, a cheerful sparrow-sized bird with red cheeks and a punk haircut, and the happy calls of the various types of laughingthrushes. Black kites are a regular sight, even in the middle of the city, and are the most common raptor seen. If you are lucky, you could spot colourful male sunbirds, ospreys or even giant white-bellied sea eagles.

Bird lovers might consider taking a break from walking to visit Mai Po Nature Reserve in the north-east of Hong Kong (www.wwf.org.hk/en/wetlands/mai-po), although please note that a permit is required. Among the species to be seen here are black-faced spoonbills; formerly critically endangered and now a protected species, 20 per cent of the world population overwinters in Hong Kong.

For further reading, check out *A Naturalist's Guide to the Birds of Hong Kong* by Ray Tipper.

## Animals

In such a densely populated territory, you would not expect much wildlife. However, thanks to the varied habitats and conservation efforts, there are chances to see unfamiliar species such as leopard cat, barking deer, pangolin, porcupine, mongoose and otter.

Rhesus and long-tailed macaque monkeys were introduced around Kowloon and Shing Mun Reservoirs (see Wilson Trail, Section 6), but, due to overpopulation, contraception is being trialled. Avoid looking

Red-base jezebel; male Indian fritillary

at them directly, since this is viewed as a threat and may lead to aggressive behaviour.

It is quite common to see disturbed soil caused by wild boars, although, being mainly nocturnal, they are rarely encountered.

### Snakes

Amphibians and reptiles are around, if seldom seen. There are fourteen venomous species of snake, eight potentially lethal, and without detailed knowledge they are very difficult to differentiate from non-venomous snakes. Although death from snakebite is incredibly rare, it is best to avoid them.

### Cattle and buffalo

Widely seen, cattle and buffalo are the feral descendants of beasts of burden used for ploughing, not dairy. They are not domesticated and injuries to walkers have been reported, therefore it is best to keep your distance.

### Butterflies, dragonflies and damselflies

As there are over 230 species of butterflies, they are frequently seen. The streams, ponds, swamps and wetlands are ideal conditions for the 107 species of dragonflies and damselflies.

### PLANTS AND FLOWERS

During World War 2 almost all vegetation was destroyed, used as fuel and building materials. Thereafter, secondary vegetation has transformed the denuded land into a green haven. With its humid subtropical climate and temperate conditions, Hong

Kong has a diverse variety of vegetation, including low-level woodland, low-level and montane forests, shrublands, grasslands and coastal areas with mangroves.

Viewing the swathes of Chinese silvergrass (*Miscanthus sinensis*) is a popular activity in Hong Kong (see Lantau Trail, Section 2). Many walks pass through tunnels of bamboos such as *Arundinaria*. Forests and woodland are mostly evergreen; some are rainforest-like due to the humid conditions, with ferns, epiphytes and aerial roots. Other human activities have contributed to the greenery, for example *feng shui* woodlands (see Lantau Trail, Section 5) and slope maintenance (see MacLehose Trail, Section 10).

The beautiful orchid tree (*Bauhinia blakeana*, see MacLehose Trail, Section 10) is most commonly seen in urban recreational areas, country parks and along catchwaters. Other favourites include the red cotton tree (*Bombax ceiba*), native to southern China, with dramatic red flowers on naked branches in early spring, and the banyan tree, with its extensive ground and aerial roots.

Found commonly on the hillsides because it is tenacious, withstanding torrential rain and typhoons, is the fried egg plant (*Polyspora axillaris*), an evergreen native shrub with white flowers and yellow stamens. Camellia tends to be found on mountaintops, and can be seen flowering from winter to early spring. There are 10 species in Hong Kong, including the tea-making variety *Camellia sinensis*.

Named as 'King of all flowers' in China, the azaleas blossom and cover the hillsides in spring, in hues ranging

Miscanthus sinensis *in flower*

from pale pink to red. There are six native species in Hong Kong, including the Hong Kong azalea (*Rhododendron hongkongense*) and the red azalea (*Rhododendron simsii* Planch.), both of which are commonly seen, especially on Ben Nevis (Walk 4).

## HISTORY

After its beginning as a volcano, the area has been inhabited from the Palaeolithic era, becoming part of the Chinese Empire in 221BC as a minor fishing port. It stayed a tranquil backwater for millennia. In 1839, Britain went to war with the Chinese Empire to force it to import British opium; Britain wanted to even out the balance of trade, which was heavily in China's favour as tea had become a popular British beverage and China required payment in silver, which the British did not have. At the end of the First Opium War, Hong Kong was ceded to Britain at the Treaty of Nanjing in 1842. Kowloon was ceded at the end of the Second Opium War in 1860, and then, as trade expanded, the New Territories were leased in 1898 for 99 years. During World War 2, the entire area was occupied by the Japanese from 1941 to 1945.

Over the next few decades, especially during the Chinese Civil War (which ended in 1949) and the Cultural Revolution (1966–76), there was a rapid influx of people into Hong Kong, seeking a place to live and trade. This was the catalyst of the transformation into today's metropolis. In theory, the British government could have returned only the New Territories at the end of the lease in 1997; however, the end result of prolonged negotiations was the return of the whole of Hong Kong to the People's Republic of China, with their promise of 'one country, two systems', whereby capitalism and political freedom are allowed to continue.

Since then, there has been intermittent unrest and demonstrations, with extensive protests in 2019–20. National Security Law was introduced in June 2020.

For a far more detailed review of Hong Kong's history, visit the excellent Hong Kong Museum of History for free (www.lcsd.gov.hk).

## RELIGION

The largest religions are Buddhism and Taoism, each having major temples. Many of the smaller local temples encountered on walks are of the uniquely Hong Kong blend of the two, with added Confucianism. Often seen are statues of Bodhisattva (Buddhist saints, usually female), including the massive 76m-tall one at Tsz Shan Monastery near Tai Po, visible from afar. Hong Kong has religious freedom, with all major religions represented.

## GETTING THERE

Hong Kong International Airport is the only international airport in Hong Kong. It is an important travel hub, with many major airlines flying there from all over the world. There are direct flights from key cities in Europe, the USA, Canada, Asia, Australia and South Africa.

From the UK, direct flights operate from Heathrow, Gatwick and Manchester with the following airlines: Cathay Pacific (www. cathaypacific.com), British Airways (www.britishairways.com), and Virgin Atlantic (www.virginatlantic.com). There are indirect flights from all major UK airports.

Easy onward transport is available from the airport to all parts of Hong Kong.

### Visa

British citizens whose passports have at least six months' validity can enter Hong Kong for a period of up to 180 days without a visa. Citizens of most European countries, Australia, Canada and the USA can visit Hong Kong visa-free and stay for up to 90 days. For further information, please consult the Hong Kong Immigration Department website (www.immd. gov.hk/eng/services/visas/visit-transit/ visit-visa-entry-permit.html).

### Vaccination

No special vaccination or malaria prophylaxis are required, although hepatitis A vaccination is recommended.

## GETTING AROUND

Hong Kong is blessed with one of the best transport systems in the world, enabling you to travel easily, cheaply and extensively around the area. The easiest option is to use an Octopus card, a pre-loaded cashless card valid on all Mass Transit Railway (MTR) routes, buses, green mini-buses, ferries and trams. You can buy and top up Octopus cards from most convenience stores and MTR stations as well as at the Airport Express desk. Either get a tourist Octopus card (HK$39, non-refundable) or an on-loan Octopus card (HK$50, refundable).

Simplified public transport options are provided for accessing and leaving all the walks in this guide, although there will be multiple other options depending on your base and preferences. The Transport in Hong Kong web page is a useful resource (www.td.gov.hk/en/transport_in_ hong_kong), and the 'HKeMobility' app with online journey planner (www.hkemobility.gov.hk) provides comprehensive travelling options and travel news. With extremely limited parking and congested roads, self-driving is not recommended.

There is a bewildering array of public transport options, and most of them have their individual apps to help with journey planning, even giving the estimated arrival time of the next train or bus. Contact details for the major providers can be found in Appendix A.

### Mass Transit Railway

The Mass Transit Railway (MTR) covers most of Hong Kong, both under- and overground. Stations are huge, so this guide will tell you exactly which exit to use to begin the walks or to catch a bus to reach your destination. Note that Central and Hong Kong MTR stations are linked with an underground tunnel. Routes can be planned using the website www.mtr.com.hk, or download the app 'MTR Mobile'.

### Bus

Buses are air-conditioned and plentiful, and cover most of Hong Kong. Final destinations are prominently displayed in both English and Chinese at the front of the bus. Payment is by Octopus card or cash (you will need the exact change). For bus timetables and other information:

- Kowloon and the New Territories: Kowloon Motor Bus (www.kmb.hk/en or 'APP 1933-KMB/LWB' app)
- Hong Kong Island: New World First Bus and City Bus (www.bravobus.com.hk/home or 'CitybusNWFB' app)
- Lantau Island: New Lantau Bus (www.nlb.com.hk or 'New Lantao Bus' app) and Long Win Bus serving north Lantau Island and the airport (www.lwb.hk/en or 'APP 1933-KMB/LWB' app).

### Minibus

Minibuses are small buses carrying up to 19 people, and they will not stop when full. Green minibuses operate along a specific route with designated stops; payment is by Octopus card or cash (the exact change is required). Red minibuses have no designated stops and passengers can get on and off along the route; payment is by cash only (again, exact change required).

The ability to speak Cantonese is almost a prerequisite to travel on minibuses, as is knowing exactly where to get off. For this reason, they are avoided where possible in this guide, unless there is no other option or the start and end are both termini. See www.16seats.net/eng/index.html.

Beware that bus and minibus numbers do not match. Similarly, different regions use different numbering systems. Passengers are required by law to wear seat belts when one is available.

### Taxi

There are three types of taxis (all of them metered) depending on the area they serve:

- **Red:** operates throughout most of Hong Kong except on Lantau Island
- **Green:** operates in the New Territories
- **Blue:** operates only on Lantau Island.

Passengers are required by law to wear seat belts.

A kaito (small ferry) is used to access Walk 18

**Ferry**
There are various licensed and franchised ferry operators. Payment is by Octopus card or cash (the exact change is required). Ferry information, including websites, is provided for individual walks in this guide; for general information, please see www. td.gov.hk/en/transport_in_hong_kong/ public_transport/ferries/index.html.

| WEATHER AND WHEN TO GO |

Hong Kong has a humid subtropical climate with mild winters and hot sticky summers. In January and February, temperatures are usually 15–20°C, with occasional drops to below 10°C when there is a cold front. Sub-zero temperatures and frost are rare but can occur on high ground and in rural areas. Wildflowers, including azaleas and rhododendrons, bloom in the milder temperatures of March and April; the weather is more humid during these months, with fogs and drizzle.

Temperatures from May to September are the hottest, at over 30°C, with chances of thunderstorms, typhoons and heavy rainfall. This is mostly too hot for walking, but you can choose more shaded routes, especially ones which include walking by beaches with swimming opportunities. Beware of stormy weather, leading to flooding, flash floods and landslides. High temperatures may cause heat stroke and dehydration (see 'Health and safety').

Average temperatures from late October to December are 20–25°C,

21

with breezes and plenty of sunshine, and it is dry in terms of both rainfall and humidity, making ideal conditions for hiking. November and December are the best months for viewing swathes of golden *Miscanthus sinensis* swaying in the mountains; however, the dry weather increases the risk of hill fires.

It is always wise to check the weather before setting off for your hiking trip. For weather forecasts and warnings of typhoons, rainstorms and fire risk, consult the Hong Kong Observatory website: www.hko.gov.hk/en/. Hiking when rainstorm or typhoon warnings are in place is not recommended.

## ACCOMMODATION

A huge range of holiday accommodation is available, from youth hostels and budget hotels to luxurious five-star options.

There are 41 government campsites in the country parks. Wild camping is not permitted. To prevent hill fires, it is illegal to light a fire when the fire risk is red, and only at designated barbecue sites and campsites. Where campsites are available near the long-distance trails, they are shown in a table in the introduction to the trail. Booking is not required; it is first come first served, with no charge.

There are two non-government campsites on MacLehose Trail. For details, see the websites listed under 'Camping and accommodation' in Appendix A.

Note that water supplies at campsites may be unreliable, the water is often untreated, and hygiene facilities are basic. Please see the Agriculture, Fisheries and Conservation Department website for further information: www.afcd.gov.hk.

## LANGUAGE

English is widely spoken, but not universal. The most common dialect is Cantonese; this is different from Mandarin (also called Putunghua), the official spoken language of China, although they are written the same. Signs and public announcements are usually in Chinese and English. A glossary of useful phrases is provided in Appendix B.

## MONEY

The unit of currency is the Hong Kong dollar (HKD). A dollar is divided into 100 cents, although cents have so little value that no one uses them any more.

| Exchange rates (spring 2022) | |
| --- | --- |
| | **Hong Kong dollars** |
| 1 British pound | 10.31 |
| 1 euro | 8.66 |
| 1 US dollar | 7.82 |

Coins are in denominations of $1, $2 and $5; banknotes are $10, $20,

$50, $100, $500 and $1000. Avoid carrying $1000 notes, as it is not easy to get change.

Credit cards are widely accepted, but not for transport. For bus, minibus and ferry travel, payment is in cash (using the exact change only) or by Octopus card.

## MOBILE PHONES AND INTERNET

Many walks are in areas with poor or absent mobile phone signal. Some walks are very close to the mainland Chinese border, so be careful not to incur roaming charges. Tourist mobile SIM cards are for sale at the airport, convenience stores and various mobile phone company stores. Internet access is widely available: at the airport (free), in hotels, some shopping malls and restaurants, and on some public buses (free).

## TIPS ON WALKING IN HONG KONG

It is best to start early to get quieter public transport and to avoid running out of daylight (sunset in midsummer is around 7pm and in December is before 6pm).

Hong Kong is a highly safety-conscious place, so you may see overcautious warning signs such as 'experienced walkers only' or 'beware of dehydration and heat exhaustion'. We have hiked all the walks in this book to ensure they are appropriate, and have graded them accordingly: see 'Using this guide'.

'Leave no trace' is an ethos well embedded in the consciousness

## PRACTICALITIES

**Time:** Hong Kong is GMT +8hr, with no daylight saving.

**Electricity:** 220V AC 50Hz, with UK-style three-pin (rectangular) plugs.

**ID:** Hong Kong residents carry their ID cards by law; visitors should carry their passports.

**Public holidays:** Hong Kong has 17 public holidays but you would be hard-pressed to notice any difference in the hustle and bustle, as most places and public transport all work as normal. Hiking trails can be busy during public and school holidays, so avoid very popular walks at these times. Shops, restaurants and public transport usually operate seven days a week.

**Foreign travel advice:** Please check on the UK government website regarding travelling to Hong Kong (www.gov.uk/foreign-travel-advice).

of most walkers. Do not feed wild or feral animals. Do not light fires except in designated areas; not only are they illegal, but they could cause hill fires. Full rules for walking in the nature parks can be found on the Agriculture, Fisheries and Conservation Department website: www.afcd.gov.hk.

## WHAT TO TAKE

- Good comfortable boots that you have worn before are essential.
- Sun protection is necessary at all times, including when the sun is completely covered by cloud: use SPF50 plus a wide-brimmed hat.
- Wearing long trousers and long-sleeved T-shirts is useful because vegetation can be scratchy, plus it helps to prevent insect bites.
- Lightweight waterproofs are helpful as a windbreaker, for extra warmth, or in case of unexpected torrential downpours.
- Proper walking socks of the appropriate grade are worth every penny.
- Walking poles protect the knees on descents, of which there are many.
- An umbrella is surprisingly effective at reducing the depredations of the midday sun, and the locals use them.
- An emergency kit should be carried, for example containing whistle, first-aid kit, space blanket, snack bars, battery bank, Swiss army knife, torch, and spare bootlaces.

## WATER

Tap water is officially drinkable, but most locals boil it. Carry plenty of water, up to one litre per person per hour when the temperature is over 30°C, and consider substituting it with an electrolyte-rich sports drink when over 40°C. You can carry less by drinking more before and after. Note that in public toilets there may be no water or only untreated water.

## WAYMARKING

Routes tend to have good signage. The long-distance trails and country trails all have their own signs, although, as they are similar, caution is required when routes cross.

*That's a lot of signs! (Walk 3)*

Be careful of following ribbons: they may represent a route but not necessarily the one you want.

## MAPS AND GPS

For hiking, it is best to use the five 1:25,000 scale Countryside Series Maps published by Hong Kong Survey and Mapping Office Lands Department:

1   Lantau Island & Neighbouring Islands
2   North West New Territories
3   North East & Central New Territories
4   Hong Kong Island & Neighbouring Islands
5   Sai Kung & Clear Water Bay

The maps are available to buy from Map Publications Centre, 23rd floor, North Point Government Offices, 333 Java Road, North Point (MTR Quarry Bay station, exit C) or their more convenient district offices in Central, Wan Chai and Yau Ma Tei. Please refer to the following link for their addresses and office hours: www. landsd.gov.hk/mapping/en/pro&ser/ outlet.html. Maps are also available at major post offices, although their stocks are often incomplete. Digital mapping is not available.

Please note that the red dotted paths marked as 'difficult/indistinct' on these maps are not always passable, and some tracks on online maps do not exist on the ground.

GPX files for every route in this book can be accessed via the Cicerone website: see 'Using this guide'. Using a free smartphone app is recommended, with roaming turned off and maps downloaded beforehand to avoid any extra charges (using the GPS function abroad is free). Always carry a paper map and compass. GPS is also useful on bus journeys, to help you get off at the correct stop.

## HEALTH AND SAFETY

Dengue fever is an infectious disease spread by the bite of *Aedes albopictus* mosquito, which is mainly active by day. There is no vaccination or specific treatment. Prevention is by insect bite avoidance, namely long-sleeved clothing and full-length trousers with liberal use of insect repellent.

Heat stroke or exhaustion is best avoided by sunscreen protection, good hydration, wearing light clothing, and not walking if the temperature is 40°C or more. If you are unwell, short of breath or have a headache, then rest in shade.

In general, it is safer not to walk alone. If walking unaccompanied, it is good practice to inform someone where you are going and when you will be back. The most likely injuries are blisters, sunburn and bee stings, so in addition to the usual dressings, be sure to have antihistamines, painkillers and blister treatments in your first-aid kit. Prevent blisters by wearing comfortable boots, drying your feet during rest stops when they are

*The ridge walk snaking fantastically onwards (Walk 7)*

hot and sweaty, and changing into dry socks if they are wet for any reason.

It is incredibly rare to be bitten by a snake, as they are scared of people, but they may bite if disturbed. If you are unlucky enough to be bitten, seek help and try not to move.

### EMERGENCIES

Contact the local police, ambulance service, fire department and other emergency services by calling 999. In Hong Kong, your call will be answered in Cantonese or English, since all emergency operators can speak both languages.

In an area covered solely by mainland China mobile networks, call 110. Your call will be answered in the official national language, Mandarin. The operator may speak English or be able to find someone who speaks it, but this is not guaranteed.

### USING THIS GUIDE

All the routes include how to get to and from public transport, both in the route description and in the GPX files. Throughout the guide, the relevant Chinese names and places have been translated into Chinese characters, so if you are ordering a taxi or seeking directions from locals, especially if they are not English speakers, simply point at the relevant entry in the guide. There is a glossary of useful phrases in Appendix B.

Information to help choose a route that suits your capabilities is listed in the route summary tables at the beginning of the book and in the information box at the start of each walk description. There are also statistics about optional extras and variants in the box. All times are pure walking times, with no allowance for photography, exploration, resting or eating. Until you are acclimatised, the heat and humidity will make for slower walking. Grading depends on distance, total ascent, ease of navigation and type of terrain, but as always is subjective (see 'Grading' below). Walking times and grading should be treated as a rough guide until you have walked a few of the routes and can compare with your own pace.

In route descriptions, places that appear on the accompanying maps are shown in **bold** in the text to aid navigation.

## Grading

The routes are graded as follows:

## The long-distance trails

For the serious walker, Hong Kong's four multi-day hiking trails (Hong Kong, Lantau, MacLehose and Wilson) are an indulgent enticement. All are well maintained and mostly well marked, apart from where they occasionally traverse urban areas; this is where GPS is especially useful. Each trail is marked with its own symbol. To help hikers monitor their progress, and in case of emergencies, there are distance posts every 500 metres. Cycling is not allowed on any of the long-distance trails.

The official sections are for administrative convenience rather than of any practical use for walkers, and some sections are short. In this guide, each trail is presented in chunks of reasonable size, joining and modifying the sections where necessary, with emphasis on ease of access via public transport. It is possible to do most sections individually, and each stage of our suggested itinerary can be done as a day walk. The trails

| | Distance (km) | Ascent (m) | Navigation | Terrain |
|---|---|---|---|---|
| **Easy** | up to 8 | up to 400 | easy | good paths |
| **Moderate** | up to 15 | up to 600 | mostly easy, with a few difficult turns | some uneven and muddy paths |
| **Difficult** | up to 20 | up to 1000 | some areas with no landmarks and paths are not clear | a lot of uneven and muddy paths |
| **Challenging** | over 20 | over 1000 | difficult | no paths, some scrambling |

can be done faster or slower, depending on pace, personal preference and access to transport.

There are campsites along MacLehose and Lantau Trails, but only limited camping on Wilson Trail and none on Hong Kong Trail. GPX files for all individual sections and suggested itineraries are available on the Cicerone website.

### GPX tracks

GPX tracks for all the routes in this guidebook are available to download free at www.cicerone.co.uk/1051/GPX. If you have not bought the book through the Cicerone website, or have bought the book without opening an account, please register your purchase in your Cicerone library to access GPX and update information.

A GPS device is an excellent aid to navigation, but you should also carry a map and compass and know how to use them. GPX files are provided in good faith, but in view of the profusion of formats and devices, neither the author nor the publisher accepts responsibility for their use. We provide files in a single standard GPX format that works on most devices and systems, but you may need to convert files to your preferred format using a GPX converter such as gpsvisualizer.com or one of the many other apps and online converters available.

*Waymarking for (clockwise from top left) Hong Kong Trail; MacLehose Trail; Wilson Trail; Country trail*

# LONG-DISTANCE TRAILS

On the ascent to Lantau Peak (Lantau Trail, Day 1)

# TREK 1
*Hong Kong Trail*

| | |
|---|---|
| **Start** | Tram station at The Peak 山頂纜車站 |
| **Finish** | Big Wave Bay 大浪灣 |
| **Distance** | 50km |
| **Total ascent** | 3430m |
| **Time** | 3 days (16hr) |
| **Terrain** | All on well-made paths; a mixture of stone and concrete steps, dirt and concrete paths, with minimal road and pavement |
| **Map** | Hong Kong Island & Neighbouring Islands |

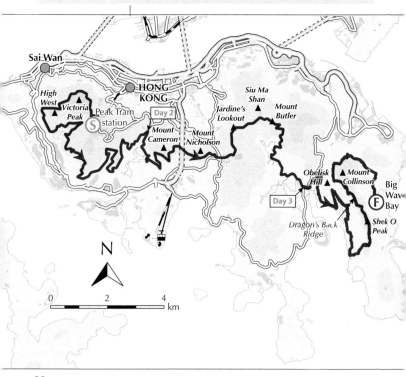

Hong Kong Trail traverses the entire length of the island and is not the concrete-surrounded route that most would imagine. Completing this 50km long-distance footpath from west to east via five country parks brings you peaks, views and nature in unexpected abundance. It is excellently designed and easy to follow, yet a challenge because of the hilly landscape. The eight sections are surprisingly varied: Section 1 is best for views, and

*The heart of Hong Kong from The Peak (Day 1)*

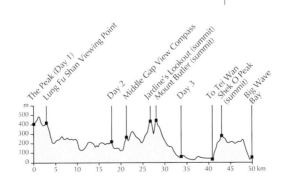

Section 8 includes the justifiably famous Dragon's Back ridge, finishing at a perfect beach. Combining Sections 7 and 8 gives a very different perspective to the undulating hills and panoramic views, adding a quiet stroll along a catchwater (see 'About Hong Kong' in the Introduction).

It is difficult to believe, in places, that this is Hong Kong main island, as you walk through dense undergrowth between giant bamboos and across trickling streams. At times there are no signs of human existence bar the beaten earth path beneath your feet.

In 2013, Hong Kong Trail was awarded the accolade of the tenth best city hiking trail in the world by Lonely Planet.

**Suggested itinerary**
The entire trail can be walked according to our suggested itinerary below, or tailored to your own personal preference, stamina and pace of walking. Each day in the itinerary can be treated as a day walk.

There is no accommodation within walking distance of the start/finish points, and camping along the trail is not permitted. Given the superbly efficient transport system, it is easy to return to a fixed base after walking. Anywhere on the island near an MTR station would be convenient, or indeed anywhere in the territory if changing trains doesn't sound arduous. Food and drink are only available at the beginning and end of the trail.

In the following table:
- The figures for **each individual section** include the trail itself plus transit to and from public transport at the beginning and end of the section.
- **Each daily total** includes transit to and from public transport at the beginning and end of the day (but does not include transit for intervening sections).
- The **overall grade for each day** takes into account cumulative distance and ascent (so although each individual section may be easy if done on its own, when combined with other sections the difficulty is likely to increase).

| Stage | Sections | Distance | Ascent | Time | Grade | Note |
|-------|----------|----------|--------|------|-------|------|
| Day 1 | 1 | 7.2km | 500m | 2hr 30min | easy | |
| | 2 | 6.6km | 410m | 2hr | easy | |
| | 3 | 7.3km | 650m | 2hr 30min | easy | |
| | **Total** | **18km** | **1400m** | **5hr 45min** | **difficult** | |
| Day 2 | 4 | 7.5km | 500m | 2hr 30min | easy | |
| | 5 | 4km | 350m | 1hr 30min | easy | no transport at section end |
| | 6 | 4.5km | 130m | 1hr 30min | easy | no transport at section start |
| | **Total** | **16km** | **980m** | **5hr 30min** | **difficult** | |
| Day 3 | 7 | 7.5km | 510m | 2hr | easy | |
| | 8 | 8.5km | 540m | 2hr 45min | moderate | |
| | **Total** | **16km** | **1050m** | **4hr 45min** | **difficult** | |

*The official start of Hong Kong Trail Section 5 and Wilson Trail Section 2*

33

# DAY 1
*The Peak to Wan Chai Gap Road*

| | |
|---|---|
| **Start** | Tram station at The Peak 山頂纜車站 |
| **Finish** | Wan Chai Gap Road bus stop, Stubbs Road 灣仔峽道巴士站, 司徒拔道 |
| **Distance** | 18km |
| **Total ascent** | 1400m |
| **Grade** | Difficult |
| **Time** | 5hr 45min |
| **Terrain** | All on well-made paths; a mixture of stone and concrete steps, dirt and concrete paths, with minimal road and pavement |
| **Summits** | Victoria Peak (552m) |

This stage begins with enticing panoramic views at Victoria Peak, one of Hong Kong's most famous landmarks, and incorporates some very wild-looking scenery. To make an adventure of the start, consider taking The Peak Tram, a funicular railway built in 1888 to serve the rich and privileged.

Much of this stage is delightfully cool and shaded beneath the forest canopy. Section 1 has the best views. Section 2 is easy walking, but best linked with Sections 1 and 3 to add interest. Section 3 is very quiet and crosses some attractive burbling streams, even in the dry season.

**Public transport for Day 1**

**Beginning:** From Hong Kong MTR station (Tung Chung line) exit B1, take bus 15 or 15X from the bus terminus across the road to the right; or take The Peak Tram (see Appendix A).

**To finish at Section 1/2 junction:** Fork right, signed Pok Fu Lam Road. Walk along this pleasant path by the reservoir for 1km, reach a T-junction and turn right; the bus stop is 100 metres along on the opposite side of the road (Pok Fu Lam Reservoir Road bus stop, Pok Fu Lam Road 薄扶林水塘道巴士站, 薄扶林道). Take bus 7 to Hong Kong MTR station (Tung Chung line).

**To start at Section 1/2 junction:** From Hong Kong MTR station (Tung Chung line) exit B1, walk to the bus terminus across the road to the right; take bus 7 to Pok Fu Lam Reservoir Road bus stop, Pok Fu Lam Road 薄扶林水塘道巴士站, 薄扶林道. Head NW then almost immediately turn right (N) onto Pok Fu Lam Reservoir Road. Walk up this road for 1km, then turn right (S), signed Peel Rise.

**To finish at Section 2/3 junction:** Continue following the road (Peel Rise, although no sign) SW by the catchwater for 400 metres. Stay on the road and at the T-junction at its end, after 800 metres, turn right, downhill (S) along Aberdeen Reservoir Road. Go straight on at the crossroads with Tsung Man Street/Yue Fai Road, then first left onto Aberdeen Main Road. Yue Fai Road bus stop 漁暉道巴士站 is 100 metres along. Take bus 7 to IFC Mall for Hong Kong MTR station (Tung Chung line).

**To start at Section 2/3 junction:** From Hong Kong MTR station (Tung Chung line) exit B1, walk to the bus terminus across the road to the right; take bus 7 to Tsung Man Street bus stop, Aberdeen Reservoir Road 崇文街巴士站, 香港仔水塘道. Head N along Aberdeen Reservoir Road for 150 metres then turn left along Peel Rise. Immediately fork right (still Peel Rise but no sign) and walk up this road for 1.2km before turning right (NE), signed Wan Chai Gap and Peak Road.

**End:** Take bus 15 to Central MTR station (Island and Tsuen Wan lines).

## Section 1

From The Peak Tram station, with your back to the exit, turn right (W), then immediately right again to Lugard Road, which is the official start of Hong Kong Trail. This rapidly becomes a pedestrianised route with amazing views. Stay on Lugard Road, which is entirely level (don't go up or down), for 2.4km to reach **High West Picnic Area**. ▸

Turn sharp right to walk along Harlech Road, following signs for Pok Fu Lam Reservoir. At the end of the concrete path 750 metres later is Pok Fu Lam Country Park. Lung Fu Shan Viewing Point is here, looking westwards towards Lantau Island on the South China Sea. Follow the crazy paving to a set of stairs on the far side and go down for about 100 metres. Then at a T-junction

Allow extra time for this section for the superlative views that change as the route winds around the summit, accompanied by fascinating information boards.

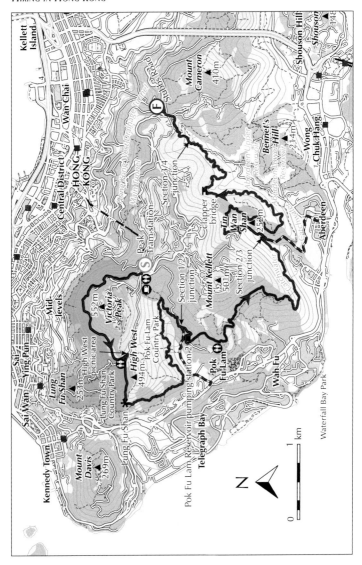

## VICTORIA PEAK

Victoria Peak, regarded as the symbol of the 'Pearl of the Orient', is the highest peak on Hong Kong Island, with a commanding view overlooking the harbour, and was the site of the colonial governor's residence.

The old name, documented in the Qing Dynasty, was 硬頭山, meaning Hard Head Hill. Legend had it that after the famous pirate Cheung Po Tsai (see Walk 16) was defeated, the Hongkongers, mainly fishermen, believed that the territory would become peaceful, hence the name was changed to 太平山, meaning Peaceful Hill.

After colonisation, the name was changed officially three times: first, to Mount Possession, then Mount Austin, and finally Victoria Peak. The locals did not like the literal translation of the latter, so the Chinese name was changed to 扯旗山, meaning Raising the Flag Peak. Nobody knows the exact origin, whether it is linked to raising the flag when the British colonised Hong Kong, the use of flags by seafarers for naval navigation, or flags used in meteorology to measure wind speed. More importantly, however, most Hongkongers past or present would simply call it The Peak.

turn left. Continue on the main path, wonderful and shaded, ignoring any of the few turnings off the path, now following signs for Chi Fu (not to the reservoir).

The next 3km are amazing: despite being on Hong Kong Island, one of the most populous places in the world, here the route traverses dense undergrowth between thick clumps of bamboos and crosses trickling streams. Get to a road and turn right, downhill; 150 metres later is a fork, which is the **Section 1/2 junction**. To continue the trail, fork left, following signs for Peel Rise.

### Section 2
About 400 metres from the Peel Rise turn, walk past **Pok Fu Lam Reservoir**

*The iconic Peak Tower*

*Banyan tree tunnel*

It is bizarre to see a 'beware of horse' sign here. This was a bridle path for the British gentry in colonial times, and there is still a riding school nearby.

**pumping station 2**. Shortly after, with a picnic area on the right, turn left up some steps, still following signs for Peel Rise. At a concrete road 200 metres later, go left, signed Chi Fu. This ends after 400 metres at a T-junction; turn left again, following signs for Peel Rise. ◄

Follow the main path for about 2km to the end of concrete, with amazing views of Lamma Island on the right. Go down some steps to a shelter and straight on at a footpath crossroads. At a fork 200 metres later, go left, signed Peel Rise. Follow this down many stairs (not taking any turnings) for 300 metres. At the bottom, cross over the catchwater to a T-junction and go left to walk along it (no sign) for about 1km. Shortly after a large dam-like structure is a road junction; this is the **Section 2/3 junction**. To continue the trail, turn left (NE) along this road (which is Peel Rise, although no signs), signed Wan Chai Gap and Peak Road.

**Section 3**
Continue NE along Peel Rise for 600 metres, then at a path crossroads (with a picnic area and shelter on the left), go right, signed Wan Chai Gap. This is another one of those sections where the sight and sound of the city have completely vanished, as the route crosses over a pretty river. At a junction 1.6km later, go straight ahead, signed Aberdeen Reservoir. Cross another beautiful stream via a **clapper bridge**; 2.5km after the previous junction, reach another junction and go straight ahead following signs for Wan Chai Gap (Aberdeen Reservoir is signed right).

Arrive at Aberdeen Reservoir Road 850 metres later, which is the official **Section 3/4 junction**. ▶ To finish today's itinerary, turn left following signs for Wan Chai Gap, cross a bridge and go up the road for 500 metres to Mount Cameron Road. Turn left, then turn right at the end of this road 150 metres later onto **Stubbs Road**; Wan Chai Gap Road bus stop is a further 50 metres on the left.

To continue the trail, cross the road and take a path signed Black's Link via Middle Gap Road.

# DAY 2
*Wan Chai Gap Road to Tai Tam Tuk Reservoir*

| | |
|---|---|
| **Start** | Wan Chai Gap Road bus stop, Stubbs Road 灣仔峽道巴士站, 司徒拔道 |
| **Finish** | Tai Tam Reservoir North bus stop, Tai Tam Road 大潭水塘北巴士站, 大潭道 |
| **Distance** | 16km |
| **Total ascent** | 980m |
| **Grade** | Difficult |
| **Time** | 5hr 30min |
| **Terrain** | All on well-made paths; a mixture of stone and concrete steps, dirt and concrete paths, with minimal road and pavement |
| **Summits** | Jardine's Lookout (433m), Mount Butler (435m) |

Section 4 alone is a gentle, shaded stroll through nature-filled subtropical woodland, suitable for families. There are also some World War 2 remnants.

This is followed by Section 5, where a marvellous ascent is rewarded by magnificent views into the bustling heart of Hong Kong. Note that there is little shade, so on hot days start early and bring ample water. With no public transport from the end of Section 5, it would be better joined with Section 6, an easy section with shade and vistas over several reservoirs.

**Public transport for Day 2**

**Beginning:** From Hong Kong MTR station (Tung Chung line) exit B1, take bus 15 from the bus terminus across the road to the right.

**To finish at Section 4/5 junction:** Take bus 6 or 66 from Tai Tam Reservoir Road bus stop, Wong Nai Chung Gap Road, to Central Exchange Square for Hong Kong MTR station (Tung Chung line).

**To start at Section 4/5 junction:** From Hong Kong MTR station (Tung Chung line) exit B1, walk to the bus terminus across the road to the right; take bus 6 to Wong Nai Chung Reservoir Park bus stop, Wong Nai Chung Gap Road

黃泥涌水塘公園巴士站, 黃泥涌峽道. Take the first set of steps on the left immediately after the garage, go up to Tai Tam Reservoir Road, and turn left.

**To finish or start at Section 5/6 junction:** A pre-booked taxi or private transport is required.

**End:** Take bus 14 to Sai Wan Ho Civic Centre bus stop; Sai Wan Ho MTR station (Island line) is on the opposite side of the road.

### Section 4

Head downhill and take the first right-hand turn onto Mount Cameron Road, then 150 metres later take the first right again, down Aberdeen Reservoir Road, signed Aberdeen Country Park. After 500 metres, just before a bridge, take a left-hand footpath labelled Hong Kong Trail and Lady Clementi's Ride (金夫人馳馬徑 which translates as Mrs Gold Bridle Path), following signs for Black's Link via Middle Gap Road. This is the official **Section 3/4 junction**.

Almost immediately, the trail heads through subtropical woodland surrounded by rattan, cardamom, bamboo, pandanus and many flowers, with the gentle sounds of a small river in the valley beneath. At a junction 300 metres along, stay on the main path, curving rightwards and following the same signs (ignore a left turn).

Continue along for 1.5km, with views of Aberdeen Reservoir glimpsed through the dense foliage to the right, go past a **World War 2 concrete bunker** and a picnic site to a crossroads with a shelter. Turn left, still following the same signs, now walking along a massive catchwater for nearly 1km. Turn left, crossing the catchwater, still following signs for Black's Link, then go up some steps to reach

*World War 2 bunker*

41

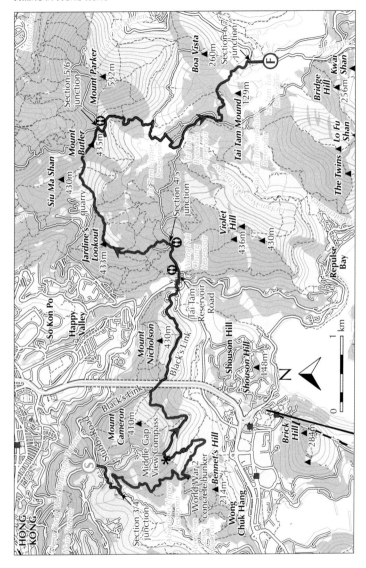

Middle Gap Road (no sign). About 600 metres up this steep ascent, turn right, signed Black's Link.

Walk past **Middle Gap View Compass** (with views of Ocean Park theme park), after which the trail becomes an enjoyable rough path. After 1.4km, reach a concrete road; this is **Black's Link** (not signed). Turn right, now following signs for Wong Nai Chung Gap for 1.75km as the path becomes a road lined with very posh houses, leading to Deep Water Bay Road. Turn left and Tai Tam Reservoir Road bus stop is 50 metres along. ▶ To continue the trail, turn right uphill just after the bus stop, along **Tai Tam Reservoir Road**.

*There are no more Hong Kong Trail signs from here until the official start of Section 5.*

### Section 5

Walk uphill for 500 metres, passing **Wong Nai Chung Reservoir**, and take the second footpath on the left after the reservoir, which is the **Section 4/5 junction**. ▶ Head N up steps on the right, following signs to Jardine's Lookout and Osborn memorial. A steep ascent of about 1.2km leads to **Jardine's Lookout 渣甸山**, with splendid views of central Hong Kong.

*There is a big archway here for both Hong Kong and Wilson Trails, but no signs before this.*

> **Jardine's Lookout** is named after William Jardine, founder of Jardine Matheson import–export company, still one of the top 200 companies in the world. In the 19th century it was used as an observation post, where a watch was kept for the firm's ships; this allowed the company to be waiting at the docks on their arrival, therefore receiving news before their competitors.

Continue for 1.2km, now following signs for Mount Butler, past a **quarry** on the left and views of Tai Tam Upper Reservoir and Tai Tam Tuk Reservoir on the right. When Wilson Trail goes left, continue straight on, having lost signs for Mount Butler but now following signs for Tai Fung Au. After 350 metres along excellent, mostly shaded paths, arrive at **Mount Butler 畢拿山**. From here, go down the 599 steps of Jacob's Ladder. ▶ Arrive at Mount Parker Road barbecue area, which is the **Section 5/6 junction**.

*In Chinese, this is 天梯, meaning Heavenly Ladder.*

*The cluster of Tai
Tam Reservoirs*

## Section 6

From the barbecue area at the bottom of Jacob's Ladder, turn sharp right (SW), following signs for Tai Tam Tuk Reservoir. Also referred to as Hong Kong Forest Track, Mount Parker section, this is a maintenance road but nice, cool and shaded. At a fork 1.5km along, go right, still following signs for the reservoir. Some 500 metres later, reach the dam of **Tai Tam Upper Reservoir** 大潭上水塘 and walk across it.

At the end of the dam, turn right (no sign) and follow the shore of the reservoir for 200 metres to a bridge. Do not cross it but continue straight ahead following signs for Tai Tam Road, walking by **Tai Tam Byewash Reservoir** 大潭副水塘. Cross the dam at its end to reach a road.

Follow the road, heading downwards for 500 metres, to a sign for Tai Tam Country Park where there are two turnings on the left. Take the second one, a lovely path signed Tai Tam Road with the Hong Kong Trail symbol. (Beware: the road straight ahead is also signed Tai Tam Road.)

Follow this path for 1.3km to Tai Tam Road 大潭道, and the official **Section 6/7 junction**. ◄ To complete today's itinerary, turn right, downhill (caution, no pavement) for 200 metres to the bus stop on this side of the road just before **Tai Tam Tuk Reservoir** 大潭篤水塘.

*To continue the
trail, go straight
ahead down the
steps, heading SE.*

# DAY 3
*Tai Tam Tuk Reservoir to Big Wave Bay*

| | |
|---|---|
| **Start** | Tai Tam Reservoir North bus stop, Tai Tam Road 大潭水塘北巴士站, 大潭道 |
| **Finish** | Big Wave Bay 大浪灣 |
| **Distance** | 16km |
| **Total ascent** | 1050m |
| **Grade** | Difficult |
| **Time** | 4hr 45min |
| **Terrain** | All on well-made paths; Section 7 is easy walking along a catchwater; Section 8 is a mixture of stone and concrete steps, plus dirt and concrete paths |
| **Summits** | Shek O Peak (284m) |

Section 7 is verdant and shaded, with many birds and butterflies and some excellent sea views. It is easy level walking and uncrowded even at weekends. Section 8, known as Dragon's Back, is the most famous walk in Hong Kong, voted Asia's best urban hike. Look forward to great ascents to hills with panoramic views of Stanley, Tai Tam Reservoirs, Shek O, and Tung Lung Island (Walk 18). Note that Section 8 tends to get very busy at weekends and bank holidays.

The trail ends at Big Wave Bay, a beautiful beach with swimming and surfing opportunities, plus shops, restaurants and facilities.

## Public transport for Day 3

**Beginning:** From Sai Wan Ho MTR station (Island line) exit A, take bus 14.

**To finish at Section 7/8 junction:** From To Tei Wan bus stop, Shek O Road (on this side of the road), take bus 9 to Shau Kei Wan bus terminus, then walk to Shau Kei Wan MTR station (Island line).

**To start at Section 7/8 junction:** From Shau Kei Wan MTR station (Island line) exit A3 (bus terminus), take bus 9 to To Tei Wan bus stop, Shek O Road 土地灣巴士站, 石澳道.

**End:** Take bus 9 or red minibus (cash only) to Shau Kei Wan bus terminus, then walk to Shau Kei Wan MTR station (Island line).

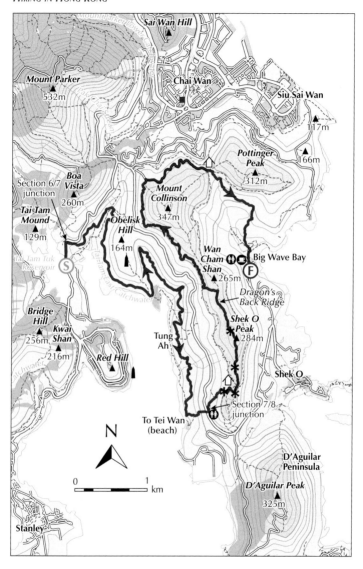

Sai Wan Hill

Mount Parker
532m

Chai Wan

Siu Sai Wan
117m

166m

Pottinger
Peak
312m

Boa
Vista
260m

Section 6/7
junction

Mount
Collinson
347m

Tai Tam
Mound
129m

Obelisk
Hill
164m

Wan
Cham
Shan
265m

Big Wave Bay

Tai Tam Tuk
Reservoir

S

Tai Tam East Catchwater

Dragon's
Back Ridge

Shek O
Peak
284m

Bridge
Hill
256m

Kwai
Shan
216m

Red Hill

Tung
Ah

Shek O

Section 7/8
junction

To Tei Wan
(beach)

N

D'Aguilar
Peninsula

0        1
km

D'Aguilar Peak
325m

Stanley

*Tai Tam Tuk Reservoir dam*

## Section 7

From the bus stop, walk uphill away from the dam (caution, no pavement) for 200 metres to the signboard at the official **Section 6/7 junction**. Take the set of steps on the right (W), going downwards. Walk along **Tai Tam East Catchwater** for 6.5km without deviation. ▶ At its end, the path becomes a lovely dirt track, then shortly afterwards go left at a T-junction, now on a concrete footpath.

> The function of the pair of **obelisks**, one on Obelisk Hill and one on Redhill Peninsula, is a mystery: most likely they were navigational, used to check ship's compasses at a fixed bearing of 355 degrees. The original wooden markers were replaced with the current 9m columns by the Royal Navy in 1910.

About 200 metres further on, turn sharp left up a set of steps signed Hong Kong Trail Dragon's Back. ▶ At the top of a lot of steps reach a road, which is the **Section 7/8 junction**. To continue the trail, cross the road and go straight up the steps.

There are views of temples on the coast at Tung Ah village 東丫村, then of the obelisks, and Stanley across the bay.

Straight ahead is a lovely little beach at To Tei Wan 土地灣, with watersport facilities.

*The Dragon's Back ridge*

**Section 8**

Go straight up the steps, concrete initially, then a lovely rough path. Pass a viewpoint 500 metres later, then 150 metres further along turn right at a **shelter**, uphill. Continue for 900 metres, past two more viewpoints, to **Shek O Peak**.

The undulating ridge of **Dragon's Back** begins at Shek O Peak (打爛埕頂山 Broken Wine Amphora Hill) and ends at the summit of Wan Cham Shan (雲枕山 Cloud Pillow Hill).

*From the viewing point, it is clear how Big Wave Bay earned its name, and it is very relaxing to watch the waves roll onto the beach.*

Walk on, now following signs for Tai Tam Gap, past Dragon's Back viewing point, and turn left down the steps 750 metres along, before **Wan Cham Shan**. ◄ At the bottom of the steps turn right. Follow this pretty, green, shaded path for about 2km, then it becomes a concrete road downhill. Shortly thereafter at a T-junction go right. Continue for 1.3km, then just after the second **shelter**, by a catchwater, turn right down some steps following signs to Big Wave Bay.

*The finish sign certainly does not look official and it says 10 sections!*

The official finish point is painted on the floor 1.5km later in the village of **Big Wave Bay**. ◄ Walk S for 600 metres to the bus stop at the end of the village.

# TREK 2
*Lantau Trail*

| | |
|---|---|
| **Start/Finish** | Mui Wo Pier 梅窩碼頭 |
| **Distance** | 73.75km |
| **Total ascent** | 4550m |
| **Time** | 5 days (25hr 30min) |
| **Terrain** | All on well-made paths; a mixture of stone and concrete steps, dirt and concrete paths, with minimal road and pavement |
| **Map** | Lantau Island & Neighbouring Islands |

Lantau Island 大嶼山 means Big Mountainous Island. In Chinese, this long-distance trek is named 鳳凰徑 (Phoenix Trail) after the island's highest peak. It circumnavigates the whole of the island and encompasses some incredibly varied terrain and sights, including five of the ten highest mountains of Hong Kong. There are multiple highlights, such as Sunset Peak (third highest mountain), Lantau Peak (second highest), Tai O village and the awe-inspiring yet serene Big Buddha at Ngong Ping. Ensure

*The phoenix sculpture at the Section 3/4 junction (end of Day 1/ start of Day 2)*

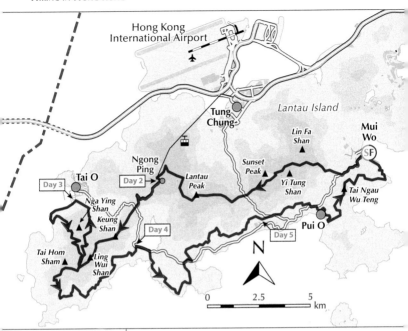

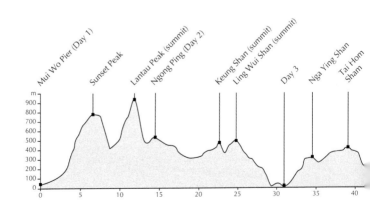

you factor in an hour or so for exploration of this astounding statue, along with Po Lin Monastery and the Wisdom Path, at the end of Section 3 or beginning of Section 4.

Section 7 is rugged and remote, significantly quieter than the marvellous summits of Sections 2 and 3, and wild enough to see dolphins and white-bellied sea eagles. Previously a hard-to-reach destination, now easily accessible thanks to MTR, bus and ferry, this is some of the best hiking that Hong Kong has to offer.

**Suggested itinerary**
With Hong Kong's superb transport system, it is relatively easy to reach the different sections of the trail. The entire trail can be walked according to our suggested itinerary below, or tailored to your own personal preference, stamina and pace of walking. Each day in the itinerary can be treated as a day walk. Options to avoid Section 1 (which is entirely on road) and to increase the challenge by adding extras are given in the route description.

Apart from camping (see campsites listed below), accommodation on or near the trail is limited to Mui Wo and Tai O, therefore if you want to stay in comfort at the end of each day's trekking, use of public transport

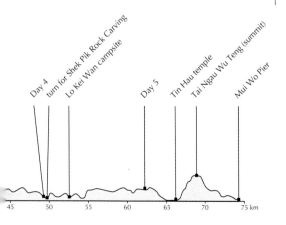

HIKING IN HONG KONG

is required. In this case, the most convenient base would be near Tung Chung MTR station or Mui Wo Pier, as the buses giving access to all sections depart from the nearby bus termini. Food and drink are only available at Mui Wo, Ngong Ping, Tai O and Pui O.

In the following table:

- The figures for **each individual section** include the trail itself plus transit to and from public transport at the beginning and end of the section.
- **Each daily total** includes transit to and from public transport at the beginning and end of the day (but does not include transit for intervening sections).
- The **overall grade for each day** takes into account cumulative distance and ascent (so although each individual section may be easy if done on its own, when combined with other sections the difficulty is likely to increase).

| Stage | Sections | Distance | Ascent | Time | Grade | Note |
|-------|----------|----------|--------|------|-------|------|
| Day 1 | 1 | 2.5km | 180m | 45min | easy | |
| | 2 | 6.5km | 780m | 2hr 45min | difficult | |
| | 3 | 5.5km | 600m | 2hr 30min | moderate | |
| | Total | 14.5km | 1560m | 6hr | challenging | |
| Day 2 | 4 | 6km | 200m | 2hr | easy | |
| | 5 | 7.5km | 450m | 2hr 45min | moderate | no public transport at section end |
| | 6 | 2.5km | 20m | 45min | easy | no public transport at section start |
| | Total | 16km | 670m | 5hr 30min | difficult | |
| Day 3 | 7 | 12.25km | 760m | 4hr 30min | moderate | no public transport at section end |
| | 8 | 5km | 260m | 1hr 30min | easy | no public transport at section start |
| | Total | 17.25km | 1020m | 6hr | difficult | |

| Stage | Sections | Distance | Ascent | Time | Grade | Note |
|-------|----------|----------|--------|------|-------|------|
| **Day 4** | 9 | 6.5km | 300m | 2hr | easy | |
| | 10 | 7.5km | 460m | 2hr | easy | |
| | **Total** | **14km** | **760m** | **4hr** | **moderate** | |
| **Day 5** | 11 | 2.8km | 120m | 1hr | easy | |
| | 12 | 9.2km | 420m | 3hr | easy | |
| | **Total** | **12km** | **540m** | **4hr** | **moderate** | |

| Campsites | | | |
|-----------|------|----------------------------------|------------|
| **Section** | **Name** | **Distance from previous campsite (km)** | **Cumulative km** |
| 2 | Nam Shan | 2.2 from start (400 metres from trail) | 2.2 |
| 4 | Ngong Ping | 13.4 | 15.6 |
| 5 | Man Cheung Po | 11.5 | 27.1 |
| 7 | Nga Ying Kok | 5.9 | 33 |
| 7/8 | Kau Ling Chung | 9.6 (500 metres from trail) | 42.6 |
| 8 | Tai Long Wan | 1.5 (350 metres from trail) | 44.1 |
| 8/9 | Shek Pik | 3.2 | 47.3 |
| 9 | Shek Lam Chau | 2.9 (400 metres from trail) | 50.2 |
| | Lo Kei Wan | 1.8 | 52 |
| 12 | Pui O | 12 (500 metres from trail) | 64 |
| | Shap Long | 2 (250 metres from trail) | 66 |
| | Pak Fu Tin | 2.6 | 68.6 |

# DAY 1
## *Mui Wo Pier to Ngong Ping*

| | |
|---|---|
| **Start** | Mui Wo Pier 梅窩碼頭 |
| **Finish** | Ngong Ping 昂坪 |
| **Distance** | 14.5km (12km without Section 1) |
| **Total ascent** | 1560m (1380m without Section 1) |
| **Grade** | Challenging |
| **Time** | 6hr (5hr 15min without Section 1) |
| **Terrain** | Section 1 is entirely on pavement adjacent to a main road; Sections 2 and 3 are on excellent dirt paths, with very many stone steps |
| **Summits** | Lantau Peak (934m); optional: Lin Fa Shan (766m), Yi Tung Shan (749m), Sunset Peak (869m) |

This stage has the most majestic peaks of the whole trail. Section 1 is all on road, so only purists who insist on walking every single step of the trail may want to complete it. To avoid the road, there is a footpath via Luk Tei Tong village, called Old Village Path.

Section 2 is justifiably the most famous and most walked section of Lantau Trail, with a wonderful ascent, but the official trail does not go to any of the summits. For this reason, three optional extra peaks are included, of which the first is the best, an away-from-it-all location with panoramic views to enjoy in solitude. Why not omit Section 1 and instead add all three extras?

Section 3 is another very popular portion of the trail, thanks to its wonderful ascent to the highest peak of Lantau Island. This has excellent stone paths, probably the best views, and ends at the serene Tian Tan Big Buddha.

**Public transport for Day 1**

**Beginning:** Take the regular ferry from Central Pier 6 (Hong Kong Island) to Mui Wo (see Appendix A). Alternatively, from Tung Chung MTR station (Tung Chung line) exit B, cross the courtyard to Tung Chung station bus terminus and take bus 3M to Mui Wo.

**To finish at Section 1/2 junction:** Walk 200 metres down the road to Nam Shan campsite bus stop then take bus 3M, 11 or 23 to Tung Chung MTR station (Tung Chung line). Nam Shan campsite is 400 metres further on the road.

**To start at Section 1/2 junction:** From Tung Chung MTR station (Tung Chung line) exit B, cross the courtyard to Tung Chung station bus terminus and take bus 3M to Nam Shan campsite bus stop 南山營地巴士站. Head E along the road and take the first left through Lantau Trail gate.

**To finish at Section 2/3 junction:** Pak Kung Au bus stop is on the opposite side of the road. Take bus 3M, 11 or 23 to Tung Chung MTR station (Tung Chung line).

**To start at Section 2/3 junction:** From Tung Chung MTR station (Tung Chung line) exit B, cross the courtyard to Tung Chung station bus terminus and take bus 3M, 11 or 23 to Pak Kung Au bus stop 伯公坳巴士站.

**End:** Take bus 23 or cable car (see Appendix A) to Tung Chung MTR station.

Lantau Island is famous for **Chinese silvergrass**, *Miscanthus sinensis* 芒草, which, although the name *sinensis* means 'from China', is native to the whole of eastern Asia. This herbaceous perennial grass has purple flowers which turn a rich golden colour in autumn. November to December is the best time to see swathes of these golden grasses swaying in the mountains of Hong Kong, especially on Lantau and Sunset Peaks or Tai Mo Shan. Viewing and taking photos of this beautiful plant has become a popular Hongkonger activity.

## Section 1

Facing away from the pier, turn right (N) and walk along the promenade to its end. There is no Lantau Trail signboard and signage is limited at the beginning. ▶ At the roundabout by Mui Wo Cooked Food Market, take the second exit along the road, heading upwards (S) signed Nam Shan. Simply walk along the road for 2.1km to

For the Old Village Path, follow signs for Lantau Trail via Silvermine Bay Beach along the coast (not described and no GPX file).

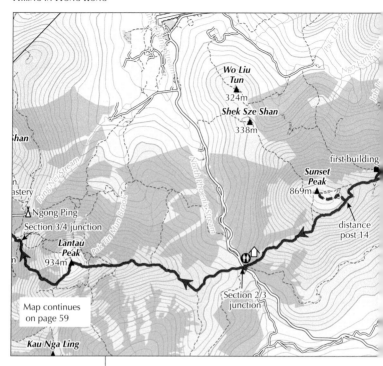

arrive at the Lantau Trail gate on the right; this is the **Section 1/2 junction**. To continue the trail, go through the gate.

### Section 2

There are many little paths but the main track is easy to follow, signed Pak Kung Au via Sunset Peak. After a long and enjoyable ascent from subtropical woodlands to grassland slopes, rewarded by amazing views, arrive at **distance post 11**, 3km from the Lantau Trail gate.

### Optional summit: Lin Fa Shan

This adds 1.4km, 150m ascent and 45min. Take the right turn by **distance post 11**. Fork right 500 metres later, and

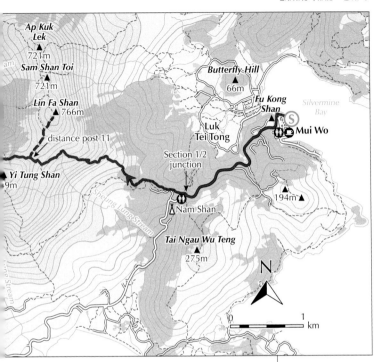

head to the obvious trig point of **Lin Fa Shan** (蓮花山 Lotus Hill). The route is quite steep, with some scrambling required. This is the sixth highest peak of Hong Kong, with amazing views, especially of Lantau Trail ahead, snaking enticingly along the awesome ridge, and of Big Buddha nestled between peaks. Retrace your steps to the route.

About 800 metres after **distance post 11** (ignore steps down on the right, signed Wong Lung Hang Road), arrive at the **first building** of many unexpected square granite structures.

The twenty or so solid buildings at **Lantau Mountain Camp** used to be a holiday resort for

*Walking back from Lin Fa Shan with the awesome ridge of Lantau Trail ahead*

Christian missionaries in the early 1920s, as before the invention of air-condition this was one of the few places to feel cool. They originally started building at the top of Hong Kong's highest mountain, Tai Mo Shan (MacLehose Trail, Section 8), but relocated here after their initial constructions were demolished by a typhoon.

**Optional summit: Yi Tung Shan**
This adds 0.8km, 50m ascent and 20min. Turn left 50 metres after the **first building**, then fork left and left again, leading to **Yi Tung Shan** (二東山 Second East Hill). This is the ninth highest peak of Hong Kong (although no marker). Retrace your steps to the route.

Follow the main track for about 600 metres from the junction with the Yi Tung Shan path and arrive at **distance post 14**.

**Optional summit: Sunset Peak**
This adds 1km, 90m ascent and 30min (although you should allow extra time to be mesmerised by the amazing

views). Turn right 25 metres after **distance post 14** and take any path to the popular summit of **Sunset Peak** (大東山 Tai Tung Shan, Big East Hill), the third highest peak of Hong Kong. Retrace your steps to the main route.

Continue along the main route, with a long descent down brilliant stone steps, arriving nearly 2km later at a **shelter**. Take the steps down to the road, which is the **Section 2/3 junction** (signboard on both sides of the road), and turn right to get past the end of the safety barriers. To continue the trail, cross the road, go left and take the first right, up steps signed Lantau Peak.

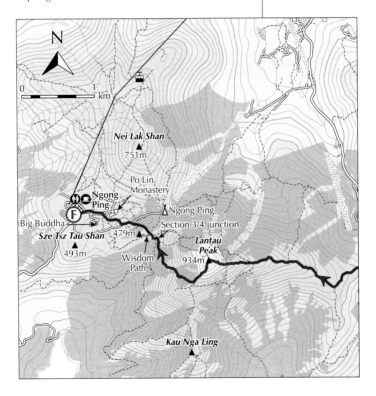

59

*A long set of steps down from Sunset Peak, looking towards Lantau Peak*

**Section 3**

Head W up the steps signed Lantau Peak. Go past a memorial to two rescue helicopter pilots, then ascend for 3km with views of many islands and beaches, arriving at **Lantau Peak** summit.

## LANTAU PEAK

Lantau Peak, the second highest peak in Hong Kong, is a double peak. In Chinese, it is aptly named 鳳凰山, meaning Phoenix Peak, as this mythical bird always comes in pairs. The views here are ample reward for the climb, taking in not only the multiple enticing summits but also the man-made structures such as Big Buddha, the airport which used to be sea, and the world's longest sea bridge–tunnel traversing 55km of the Pearl River Estuary to Macau.

*Section 4 will skirt around Nei Lak Shan.*

From the summit, go down the very long set of steps, enjoying views of Nei Lak Shan (eighth highest peak at 751m). ◄ After 1km, reach the bottom of the steps, just before which is a lovely viewpoint for the Wisdom Path

(Section 4). This is the **Section 3/4 junction**, marked with a phoenix sculpture. ▸

To continue the trail, turn right (N), signed Lantau Trail. Ngong Ping campsite is 300 metres further along.

To finish today's itinerary, go straight ahead following signs for the bus terminus, and 200 metres later fork right, still signed for the bus terminus. After a further 100 metres, reach a concrete road and turn left to walk among the many sights and facilities of **Ngong Ping**: Big Buddha statue and Po Lin Monastery, plus shops and restaurants in the village. The bus terminus is about 1km further, to the left of Ngong Ping village.

# DAY 2
## *Ngong Ping to Tai O*

| | |
|---|---|
| **Start** | Ngong Ping village 昂坪村 |
| **Finish** | Tai O bus terminus 大澳巴士總站 |
| **Distance** | 16km |
| **Total ascent** | 670m |
| **Grade** | Difficult |
| **Time** | 5hr 30min |
| **Terrain** | Begins on pedestrianised routes in Ngong Ping village, followed by dirt paths and then by a quiet road; Sections 5 and 6 are all on dirt paths |
| **Summits** | Keung Shan (459m), Ling Wui Shan (490m) |

Great walking and sightseeing can be combined in Section 4. Allow at least an hour to explore the Big Buddha, Po Lin Monastery and the Wisdom Path. There are restaurants and facilities in Ngong Ping village.

Tranquil Section 5 incorporates *feng shui* woodlands and ridge walks on open hills. It is exceptionally rural and green, and on favourable days boasts views of Macau at the end of the 55km sea bridge–tunnel. With no transport from its end, Section 5 is best joined with Section 6, a gentle stroll ending at the delightful old Tai O village, where time seems to have stood still.

**Public transport for Day 2**

**Beginning:** From Tung Chung MTR station (Tung Chung line) exit B, cross the courtyard to Tung Chung station bus terminus and take bus 23 or the nearby cable car (see Appendix A).

**To finish at Section 4/5 junction:** The correct one of the three Sham Wat Road bus stops is on the left. Take bus 11 or 23 to Tung Chung MTR station (Tung Chung line).

**To start at Section 4/5 junction:** From Tung Chung MTR station (Tung Chung line) exit B, cross the courtyard to Tung Chung station bus terminus and take bus 11 or 23 to Sham Wat Road bus stop 深屈道巴士站. From the bus stop, walk uphill to the picnic area.

**To finish or start at Section 5/6 junction:** With no roads and no public transport, it is impractical to start or finish here, therefore it is best to join Sections 5 and 6.

**End:** Take bus 11 to Tung Chung MTR station.

**Section 4**

Head towards the **Big Buddha**; from the bottom of the steps leading to the statue, take the road SE following signs for the Wisdom Path.

> The **Wisdom Path** 心經簡林 is a short sloping trail in the shape of an infinity symbol, lined with 38 giant wooden monuments. Each monument is a bisected tree inscribed with words from the centuries-old Buddhist poem the Heart Sutra.

Just before the **Wisdom Path**, opposite a shelter, is the **Section 3/4 junction**. Turn left (NE) signed Lantau Trail. Almost immediately, leave the hordes behind and stroll through impressive beautiful trees. After 300 metres (with **Ngong Ping campsite** on your right), reach a road and cross straight over. At a junction 200 metres later, turn left, heading W, signed Lantau Trail (not to Nei Lak Shan).

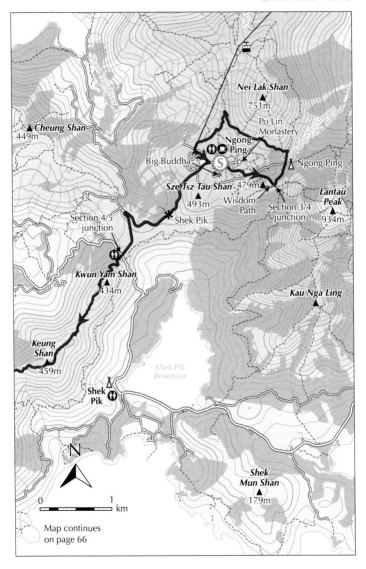

Cheung Shan
449m

Nei Lak Shan
751m

Po Lin
Monastery

Ngong Ping

Big Buddha

Ngong Ping

Sze Tsz Tau Shan
493m

479m

Wisdom Path

Section 3/4
junction

Lantau Peak
934m

Section 4/5
junction

Shek Pik

Kwun Yam Shan
434m

Kau Nga Ling

Keung
Shan
459m

Shek Pik
Reservoir

Shek
Pik

Shek
Mun Shan
179m

N

0                    1
km

Map continues
on page 66

63

## TIAN TAN BIG BUDDHA

*Tian Tan Big Buddha*

The giant bronze statue is more properly known as Tian Tan Big Buddha 天壇大佛, meaning Temple of Heaven Big Buddha. Although built and designed with modern techniques, the features are a blend of various Buddha sculptures from the pinnacle of Chinese Buddhism between AD500 and AD1000. The original idea for the Big Buddha came from the monks of Po Lin Monastery in 1973, after which it took 20 years to complete.

Continue along this section (with fantastic views of Big Buddha, Wisdom Path, the cable car and the Macau sea bridge–tunnel) for 1km to a T-junction, and turn left (S). About 600 metres later, at a T-junction beneath the **cable car cables**, turn left, then shortly afterwards reach a concrete road. Turn left then immediately right, and take the first left up a concrete ramp leading back to **Ngong Ping** village.

Head in the direction of Big Buddha and turn sharp right onto Ngong Ping Road before reaching the statue, signed Lantau Trail to Sham Wat Road. Follow the road, past the bus station, then after 1.1km arrive at **Shek Pik Viewpoint**. Go past Shan Hoi Pavilion 600 metres later and continue on the main road (Sham Wat Road)

S, downhill for 600 metres to a T-junction. This is the **Section 4/5 junction**. To continue the trail, go straight ahead into the picnic area.

### Section 5

In the picnic area, head SW past the **toilets** and up some steps signed Man Cheung Po. Ascend for 600 metres, skirt around the summit of **Kwun Yam Shan** (觀音山 Goddess of Mercy Hill) then descend for 400 metres. Begin a short but impressive ascent to a wonderful undulating ridge, and arrive 1km later at **Keung Shan** (羗山 Ginger Hill). After another 1km, at a footpath junction, turn right signed Ling Wui Shan, and almost immediately fork left.

> Look out for **feng shui woodlands** along Section 5. These flourishing woodlands are the sole remnants of long-abandoned villages, where trees were nurtured by local people in order to bring good luck and ward off evil spirits. Over time, they developed into mixed native woodlands, rich in biodiversity.

*Looking back at Goddess of Mercy Hill dwarfed by Lantau Peak*

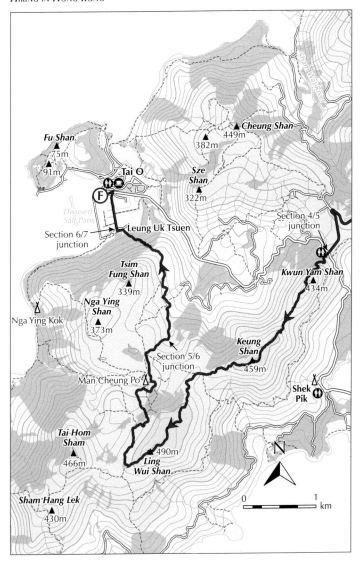

Fu Shan
75m
91m

Cheung Shan
449m
382m

Tai O

Sze
Shan
322m

Disused
Salt Pans

Section 6/7
junction

Leung Uk Tsuen

Section 4/5
junction

Tsim
Fung Shan
339m

Kwun Yam Shan
434m

Nga Ying
Shan
373m

Nga Ying Kok

Section 5/6
junction

Keung
Shan
459m

Man Cheung Po

Shek
Pik

Tai Hom
Sham
466m

N

490m
Ling
Wui Shan

0          1
km

Sham Hang Lek
430m

Continue for 1.5km to **Ling Wui Shan** (靈會山 Spirits' Gathering Hill); 400 metres thereafter in a saddle turn right (NW), signed Man Cheung Po. Walk down the valley; at the next junction, 700 metres further, go straight ahead signed Tai O via Lung Tsai. Continue along (not crossing a bridge), step over a few streams, and 1km later at a concrete crossroads go straight across, bearing leftwards (N). Pass **Man Cheung Po campsite** 200 metres later, immediately after which the path forks; go right here, heading N. At a five-way junction 300 metres further, take the second right-hand option, downhill (NE) signed Tai O via Lung Tsai. Arrive at Lung Tsai Ng Yuen Garden 600 metres later, which marks the **Section 5/6 junction**.

> **Lung Tsai Ng Yuen** (meaning Garden of Enlightenment) at Lung Tsai is a private Jiangnan garden, founded by textiles entrepreneur Wu Kun Sheng in 1962 at a cost of HK$2 million. It became dilapidated after his death, but is currently being restored.

## Section 6
Head N along the river (do not cross the dam), reach a concrete path 400 metres later, and continue in the same direction (do not go left). Almost immediately, when the concrete path bends right and downhill, go straight ahead on a rough track. Some 500 metres later, meet a concrete path and veer right, downhill, still heading N. About 1km further at **Leung Uk Tsuen** 梁屋村, reach a T-junction with another concrete path and turn left following signs for the bus terminus. There is a playground 100 metres later, and a signboard marking the **Section 6/7 junction**. ▶ To finish today's itinerary, turn right (N). After 500 metres, reach a main road and turn left; the **Tai O** bus terminus is a short distance along.

To continue the trail, fork left (W). Nga Ying Kok campsite is 2km further along the route (see Section 7).

> With stilt houses, restaurants, and shops selling the famous traditional salted fish and shrimp paste, the fishing village of **Tai O** harks back to how most of Hong Kong used to be. The locals are still mainly fishermen. The stilts used for anchoring boats had

metal roofs added, creating shelters, which were later transformed into houses.

This westernmost point of Hong Kong is well worth exploring. It is possible to stay here in the Grade 2-listed Old Police Station, now a boutique hotel, or take a boat trip searching for the critically endangered Chinese white dolphins (which are actually pink).

# DAY 3
## *Tai O to Shek Pik*

| | |
|---|---|
| **Start** | Tai O bus terminus 大澳巴士總站 |
| **Finish** | Sha Tsui bus stop, Keung Shan Road, Shek Pik 沙咀巴士站, 羌山道, 石壁 |
| **Distance** | 17.25km |
| **Total ascent** | 1020m |
| **Grade** | Difficult |
| **Time** | 6hr |
| **Terrain** | Begins on concrete paths, followed by dirt paths and many steps; finishes along a catchwater |
| **Summits** | Optional: Nga Ying Shan (374m), Tai Hom Sham (466m) |

Section 7 of Lantau Trail has been diverted indefinitely since 2013, due to the purchase of Yi O Kau Tsuen village by a private landowner. This has done walkers a favour: the diversion is a great path, starting with excellent stone steps that lead to fantastic views from several high vantage points. The tranquil scenery is beautiful, showing nature in all her majesty. Despite the large amount of ascent, Section 7 feels surprisingly easy, possibly due to the wonderful distractions, and there are some enjoyable optional extras.

With no road access at the end of Section 7, it has to be joined with Section 8, which is a pleasant, easy walk along a catchwater with possible diversions to a couple of campsites and beautiful beaches.

## Public transport for Day 3

**Beginning:** From Tung Chung MTR station (Tung Chung line) exit B, cross the courtyard to Tung Chung station bus terminus and take bus 11.

**To finish or start at Section 7/8 junction:** With neither road access nor public transport, it is best to link Sections 7 and 8.

**End:** Take bus 11, 11A or 23 to Tung Chung MTR station.

## Section 7

From the bus stop, head E on the main road then turn first right along a road going between the football field and mangroves, signed Leung Uk (梁屋 House of the Leungs). ▸ After 500 metres, stay to the left of a playground to arrive at the **Section 6/7 junction**.

Turn right (SE) signed Man Cheung Po via Nga Ying Kok. At the first fork after 400 metres, go right along the coastline, then at another fork 150 metres later go left (same sign) and continue for 1.5km. Just before **Nga Ying Kok campsite 牙鷹角營地** is the start of the diversion (with no Lantau signs until much later). Go left up some steps signed Man Cheung Po, arriving 600 metres later at a **viewpoint**. About 1km further along from the viewpoint is an unsigned path on the left to the optional summit of Nga Ying Shan.

### Optional summit: Nga Ying Shan

This adds 0.5km, 60m ascent and 15min. Turn left onto the unsigned, unmaintained path and follow it to the summit of **Nga Ying Shan** (牙鷹山 Eagle's Tooth Peak). The path may be overgrown but the views of Sections 2–6 and Big Buddha make it worthwhile. Retrace your steps to the route.

At a T-junction 800 metres after the turning to Nga Ying Shan, turn right, signed Kau Ling Chung Catchwater. Walk down this verdant, fern-lined river valley with water burbling below you. After 400 metres, cross a beautiful

Leung Uk is also signed Fan Kwai Tong, Yim Tin Pok and Nam Chung, meaning Pond of the Foreign Ghosts (pale-skinned foreigners), Salt Field Embankment and South Spring.

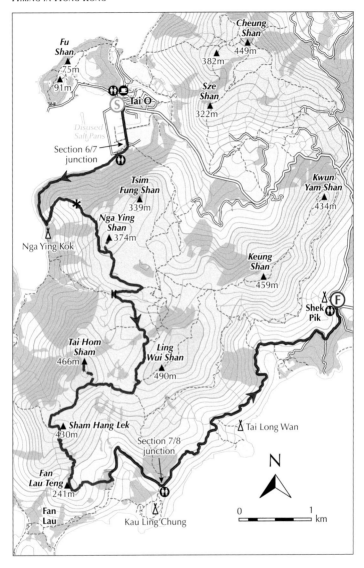

Fu Shan
75m
91m

Cheung Shan
449m
382m

Tai
Disused Salt Pans
Section 6/7 junction

Sze Shan
322m

Tsim Fung Shan
339m

Nga Ying Shan
374m
Nga Ying Kok

Kwun Yam Shan
434m

Keung Shan
459m

Shek Pik

Tai Hom Sham
466m

Ling Wui Shan
490m

Sham Hang Lek
430m

Section 7/8 junction

Tai Long Wan

Fan Lau Teng
241m

Fan Lau

Kau Ling Chung

N

0        1
km

**bridge**, then 800 metres later at a footpath T-junction turn right, now following signs for Sham Wat via Ling Wui Shan. Due to the diversion, this takes you along Section 5 of Lantau Trail, but in the opposite direction. At a T-junction 600 metres later, go right, leaving Section 5 of Lantau Trail and now following signs for Kau Ling Chung Catchwater again. Just 200 metres later at a fork, go right, signed Kau Ling Chung (W). ▶ Go up for 1km to the brow of the hill and an unsigned path on the right, where there is a second optional extra.

*Section 7 is the remotest part of Lantau Trail*

Caution: do not take the other fork, signed Kau Ling Chung (E); it is not Lantau Trail.

**Optional summit: Tai Hom Sham**
This adds 0.8km, 50m ascent and 20min. Follow the unsigned, unmaintained path to the summit of **Tai Hom Sham** (大磡森 Big Cliff Forest), with amazing views especially of the path already walked and Lantau Peak. Beware of disused mine shafts along here. Retrace your steps to the route.

Kau Ling Chung
campsite 狗嶺涌營地
is 500 metres down
a path from here.

After 1.5km, a
footpath on the right
leads to Tai Long
Wan campsite and
a small beach; the
campsite is 350
metres from the trail.

Follow the route mainly downhill for 3km, reach a
T-junction and go left, signed Shek Pik; you are now back
on the original Lantau Trail, having finished the diversion.
Just 200 metres further, reach the catchwater and turn
right, with easy walking from now on. The **Section 7/8
junction** marked by a signboard is 1.2km along. ◄

**Section 8**
Continue NE along the catchwater. ◄ Nearly 4km from
the beginning of Section 8, reach Wang Pui Road and
turn left following signs for Shek Pik. The Section 8/9
junction is at the main road 800 metres further, next to
**Shek Pik campsite 石壁營地**. Sha Tsui bus stop is on the
opposite side of the road.

# DAY 4
*Sha Tsui to Cheung Sha Catchwater*

| | |
|---|---|
| **Start** | Sha Tsui bus stop, Keung Shan Road, Shek Pik 沙咀巴士站, 羌山道, 石壁 |
| **Finish** | Cheung Sha Catchwater bus stop 長沙引水道巴士站 |
| **Distance** | 14km |
| **Total ascent** | 760m |
| **Grade** | Moderate |
| **Time** | 4hr |
| **Terrain** | Begins by the road, then mostly on concrete paths and finishes along catchwaters |

This is enjoyable, crowd-free, tranquil low-level walking on easy paths.
Section 9 is unexpectedly exceptionally pretty, with views of coastal
features, the Soko Islands (Hong Kong's southernmost), and two quiet
campsites, one on a wonderful beach. There is also the option to see a
3000-year-old rock carving. Section 10 is very relaxing, with easy walking,
mostly along tree-shaded catchwaters, and few people. If you are lucky, you
may spot an osprey or a white-bellied sea eagle.

## Public transport for Day 4

**Beginning:** From Tung Chung MTR station (Tung Chung line) exit B, cross the courtyard to Tung Chung station bus terminus and take bus 11 or 23.

**To finish at Section 9/10 junction:** Shui Hau Village East bus stop is 250 metres before the Section 9/10 junction on this side (the south side) of the road. Take bus 11, 11A or 23 to Tung Chung MTR station (Tung Chung line).

**To start at Section 9/10 junction:** From Tung Chung MTR station (Tung Chung line) exit B, cross the courtyard to Tung Chung station bus terminus and take bus 11, 11A or 23 to Shui Hau Village East bus stop 水口村東巴士站. Head E along the road, and 250 metres later is the Section 9/10 junction.

**End:** Take bus 3M, 11, 11A or 23 to Tung Chung MTR station.

## Section 9

From the bus stop near **Shek Pik campsite**, walk down the road towards the dam of **Shek Pik Reservoir** 石壁水塘. Cross it, with views of Big Buddha plus Lantau and Sunset Peaks to the left. At the other end, turn right down a road signed Shui Hau via Lo Kei Wan. After 350 metres, arrive at a fork; go left to continue the trail, and right to visit the rock carving.

*Shek Pik Rock Carving*

73

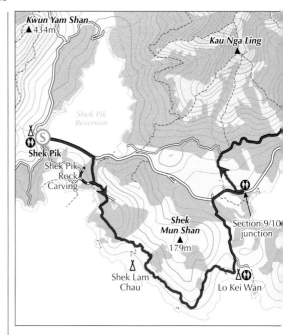

**Optional detour: Shek Pik Rock Carving**

For Shek Pik Rock Carving 石刻, turn right at the fork, following signs. Fork left again 250 metres later, and the carving is 100 metres along on the left, by the prison. After visiting the rock carving, retrace your steps to the trail.

> The Bronze Age **Shek Pik Rock Carving** is 3000 years old, consisting of geometric patterns and stylised animals. These are thought to be efforts by early inhabitants, possibly fishermen, to placate the sea gods, and may explain why more rock carvings can be found at various places around the coast (see Walks 18 and 21).

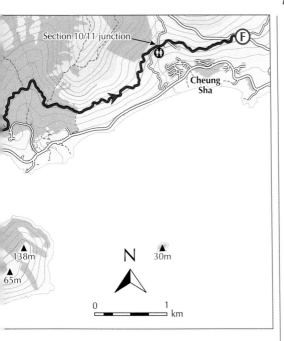

**Main route**

From the fork on the trail, follow the road for 500 metres to where it ends by a beach, then take a footpath on the left (signed Shui Hau via Lo Kei Wan). After 700 metres, pass a turning on the right for **Shek Lam Chau campsite** (石欖洲營地, 400 metres from trail), then after a further 1.8km pass another one for **Lo Kei Wan campsite** (籮箕灣營地), where there is a beautiful sheltered beach. Just 400 metres further, reach a concrete road and turn left, signed Shui Hau. About 1km along, reach the main road and turn right, signed Tung Chung Road via Catchwater. The **Section 9/10 junction** is 500 metres along the road.

**Section 10**

Turn left up the steps, following signs for Tong Fuk Catchwater. After 750 metres, reach the catchwater and turn right to walk along it, initially signed Tung Chung Road, and later Pui O. After 4km of easy, shaded walking, reach a road, turn left, then 50 metres later turn right to walk along Cheung Sha Catchwater. This is the official **Section 10/11 junction** but no transport is available here, therefore continue for another 1.5km. Go underneath a road then immediately take the stairs up on the right, signed Tung Chung Road bus stops. At the road, turn right and **Cheung Sha Catchwater bus stop** is on the opposite side of the road.

# DAY 5

*Cheung Sha Catchwater to Mui Wo Pier*

| | |
|---|---|
| **Start** | Cheung Sha Catchwater bus stop 長沙引水道巴士站 |
| **Finish** | Mui Wo Pier 梅窩碼頭 |
| **Distance** | 12km |
| **Total ascent** | 540m |
| **Grade** | 4hr |
| **Time** | Moderate |
| **Terrain** | Begins along a catchwater, then a quiet road followed by dirt paths |
| **Summits** | Tai Ngau Wu Teng (275m) |

Section 11 is easy walking along a beautiful, serene and shaded catchwater, while Section 12 takes you past an amazing beach and has some great views of the south-eastern coast of Lantau Island. There are excellent paths, and the trail ends back where you began in the busy town of Mui Wo, where there are food and accommodation opportunities.

**Public transport for Day 5**

**Beginning:** From Tung Chung MTR station (Tung Chung line) exit B, cross the courtyard to Tung Chung station bus terminus and take bus 3M, 11, 11A or 23.

**To finish at Section 11/12 junction:** 100 metres before Bui O Public School on the south side of the road is Lo Uk Tsuen bus stop, Pui O. Take bus 3M to Tung Chung MTR station (Tung Chung line). Alternatively, take bus 1, 2, 3M or 4 on the north side of the road to Mui Wo, followed by ferry to Central Pier 6 (Hong Kong Island).

**To start at Section 11/12 junction:** From Tung Chung MTR station (Tung Chung line) exit B, cross the courtyard to Tung Chung station bus terminus and take bus 3M to Lo Uk Tsuen bus stop, Pui O 羅屋村巴士站, 貝澳. Alternatively, take the ferry from Central Pier 6 (Hong Kong Island) to Mui Wo (see Appendix A), then bus 1, 2, 3M or 4 to the same bus stop. From the bus stop, head E for 100 metres to arrive at the official Section 11/12 junction at Bui O Public School.

**End:** Take bus 3M to Tung Chung MTR station or ferry to Central Pier 6 (Hong Kong Island).

## Section 11

▸ From the bus stop, continue down the road for 50 metres then take some steps on the left down to the catchwater; turn right to follow it NE. This may be a concrete catchwater but it is a very attractive green tunnel, shaded by trees and full of birds. At the end of the catchwater, 1.5km later, head right along a footpath signed Pui O.

About 300 metres along this beautiful quiet path, fork right down steps, reaching a concrete road 500 metres later. Turn right, downhill, leading to a road. Go left (E) signed Pui O. Follow the road for 500 metres to Bui O Public School, which is the official **Section 11/12 junction**.

Section 11 route description begins after the official start (see Section 10) to make access more convenient.

## Section 12

From the school, turn right onto Chi Ma Wan Road, signed Mui Wo via Shap Long. ▸ Walk along this quiet road for 500 metres. The road then runs parallel to a wide tidal river for 1km leading to the coast, with a view of the beautiful, long, sandy Pui O beach. Looking back, all the peaks of Section 2 can be seen, a serrated ridge of impressive dimensions, and in the distance Lantau Peak and Section 3.

After 200 metres there is a turning on the right for Pui O campsite 貝澳營地, which is 500 metres off the trail.

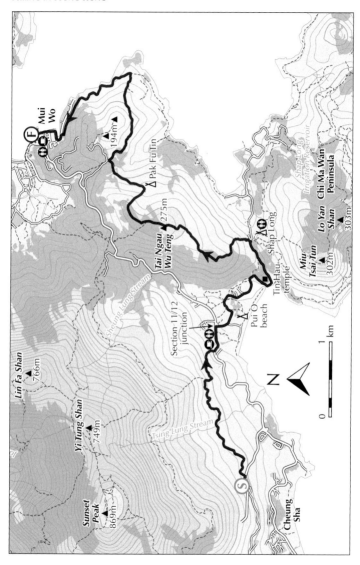

*Pui O campsite on the beautiful Pui O beach, with the ridge of Sections 2 and 3 in the background*

Pass a **Tin Hau temple** (dedicated to the Chinese Sea Goddess Tin Hau or Mazu), then the road begins to climb gently. About 800 metres later, take a footpath to the left up steps signed Mui Wo via Pak Fu Tin campsite. ▸ Follow this beautiful quiet path for 1.7km to **Tai Ngau Wu Teng**.

To the right is the path for Walk 15, and Shap Long campsite 十塱營地 is 250 metres along.

**Tai Ngau Wu Teng** 大牛湖頂 means Big Cow Lake Top. There is a helipad here and, just to the left of the route, a trig point worth diverting to for views of Lamma Island (Walks 19 and 20), Cheung Chau (Walk 16), and Hei Ling Chau Island, dotted on the silver shining sea.

About 350 metres later, fork right, signed Mui Wo via Pak Fu Tin, then 700 metres along join another path and go left down some steps. ▸ Reach a road after 700 metres, go right (SE) downhill, signed Mui Wo, then 200 metres later turn left up steps (same sign).

Pak Fu Tin campsite 白富田營地 is 60 metres to the right.

Walk along for 1.2km to a footpath crossroads and go left, still following signs for Mui Wo. About 1.5km later, on the outskirts of **Mui Wo**, fork right down steps leading to Mui Wo Ferry Pier Road. Turn left (W) and follow this for 250 metres to the promenade, then walk along it to the pier, marking the end of Lantau Trail.

# TREK 3

*MacLehose Trail*

| | |
|---|---|
| **Start** | Sai Kung Country Park Visitor Centre, Pak Tam Chung 西貢郊野公園遊客中心, 北潭涌 |
| **Finish** | Tuen Mun MTR station 屯門港鐵站 (Tuen Ma line) |
| **Distance** | 101.5km |
| **Total ascent** | 6450m |
| **Time** | 5 days (36hr) |
| **Terrain** | All on well-made paths; a mixture of stone and concrete steps, dirt and concrete paths, with minimal road and pavement |
| **Map** | Sections 1–3: Sai Kung & Clear Water Bay; Section 4 and Section 8 (first part): North East & Central New Territories; Section 8 (second part) and Sections 9 and 10: North West New Territories |

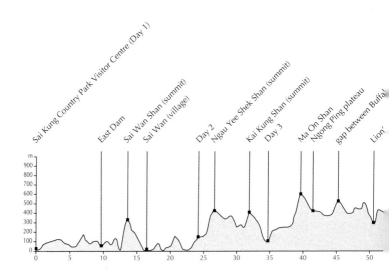

MacLehose Trail runs for over 100km from the far east to the far west of the New Territories, and is listed by National Geographic as one of the world's Dream Trails. It was named after Sir Murray MacLehose, the longest-serving governor of Hong Kong. He was a keen hiker himself and set up the country parks system, opening up a huge recreational area to the public.

The first day incorporates a visit to East Dam, a UNESCO-listed geopark with some fascinating remnants of Hong Kong's volcanic past. The eastern sections are in Sai Kung Country Parks, Hong Kong's premiere hiking destination. As the trail continues, ridge walks in its middle sections traverse imposing hills between the city of Kowloon and the New Territories, providing exceptional views high above the bustling heart of the metropolis as a contrast to the hilly rural landscape. This splendid image of the Pearl of the Orient is completed by distant views of the harbour and the famous skyscraper landscape of the northern shores of Hong Kong Island. The western

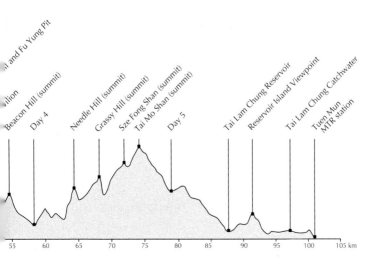

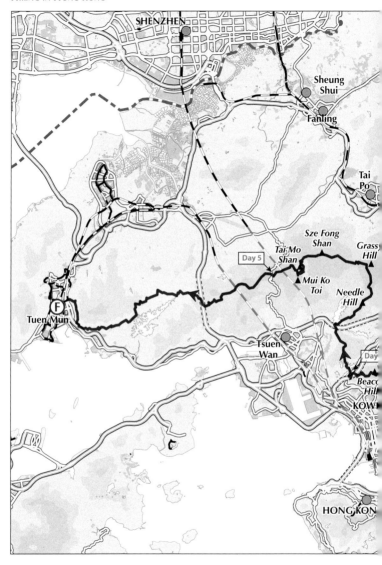

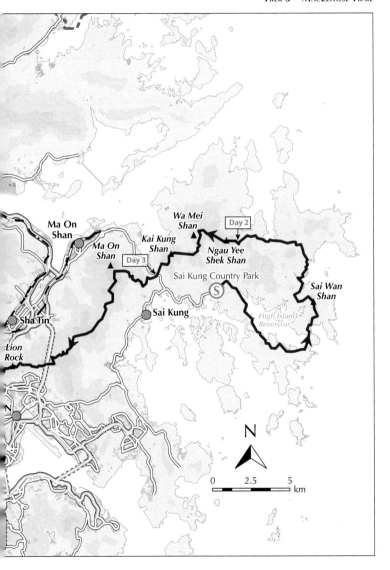

*The official start of MacLehose Trail*

sections contain many delightful reservoirs, cool and shaded, taking you past old villages linked by ancient ways, and include wonderful peaks such as Hong Kong's highest, Tai Mo Shan.

**Suggested itinerary**
With Hong Kong's superb transport system, it is relatively easy to reach the different sections of the trail. The entire trail can be walked according to our suggested itinerary below, or tailored to your own personal preference, stamina and pace of walking. Each day in the itinerary can be treated as a day walk, and the most convenient base for this would be Kowloon.

Alternatively, this would be the best trail for those who prefer to camp, as almost the whole trail is within national parks, and campsites are available. Think about both food and water when planning this option: see

'Accommodation and food' below. Other than camping and a youth hostel, there is no accommodation on or near the route and there is no baggage transfer.

Many people choose to shorten Day 1 by taking a taxi to East Dam. Not only does this avoid a long section of maintenance road, it also gives extra time for exploration of the geopark. Another option is to omit Section 1 and add Section 3 to Day 1's itinerary, making it an exceptionally long, challenging but rewarding day; the whole trail could then be completed in four days. Options to increase the challenge by adding extras are given in the route description.

In the following table:
- The figures for **each individual section** include the trail itself plus transit to and from public transport at the beginning and end of the section.
- **Each daily total** includes transit to and from public transport at the beginning and end of the day (but does not include transit for intervening sections).
- The **overall grade for each day** takes into account cumulative distance and ascent (so although each individual section may be easy if done on its own, when combined with other sections the difficulty is likely to increase).

Food and supplies are very infrequent along the trail. Most stores and kiosks sell snacks and drinks only, and although the city is in sight from the whole of Section 5, it is a long way down (and back up again).

Note that water supplies at campsites may be unreliable and the water is often untreated. For information about campsite facilities, see the Agriculture, Fisheries and Conservation Department website (www.afcd.gov.hk). For Lady MacLehose Holiday Village, see www.lcsd.gov.hk/en/camp/p_lmhv.php; for Bradbury Hall Youth Hostel (dormitories and camping), see www.yha.org.hk/en/hostels/countryside-hostels.

| Stage | Sections | Distance | Ascent | Time | Grade | Note |
|-------|----------|----------|--------|------|-------|------|
| **Day 1** | 1 | 9.75km | 410m | 3hr | easy | no transport at section end |
| | 2 | 14.75km | 930m | 5hr 30min | difficult | no transport at section start |
| | **Total** | **24.5km** | **1340m** | **8hr 30min** | **challenging** | |
| **Day 2** | **3** | **10.25km** | **670m** | **3hr 45min** | **moderate** | |
| **Day 3** | 4 | 12.75km | 960m | 5hr | moderate | no transport at section end |
| | 5 | 10.75km | 810m | 4hr | moderate | no transport at section start |
| | **Total** | **23.5km** | **1770m** | **9hr** | **challenging** | |
| **Day 4** | 6 | 5.7km | 350m | 1hr 45min | easy | |
| | 7 | 8.1km | 730m | 3hr | easy | no transport at section end |
| | 8 | 9.2km | 740m | 4hr | easy | no transport at section start |
| | **Total** | **20.75km** | **1680m** | **8hr 15min** | **challenging** | |
| **Day 5** | 9 | 6.25km | 230m | 2hr | easy | no transport at section end |
| | 10 | 16.25km | 760m | 4hr 30min | moderate | no transport at section start |
| | **Total** | **22.5km** | **990m** | **6hr 30min** | **difficult** | |

| Accommodation and food | | | | |
|---------|---------------|------|-------------------------------------|-----------------|
| **Section** | **Accommodation** | **Food** | **Distance from previous facilities (km)** | **Cumulative (km)** |
| 1 | Lady MacLehose Holiday Village | kiosk at Sai Kung Country Park Visitor Centre | at start (1km from trail) | 0 |
| | Yuen Ng Fan campsite | none | 3.3 from start (700 metres from trail) | 3.3 |
| | Po Kwu Wan campsite | none | 3.3 from start (1km from trail) | |
| | Pak Lap campsite | none | 5.2 from start (100 metres from trail) | 8.5 |
| 2 | Long Ke Wan campsite | none | 2.6 | 11.1 |

| Accommodation and food | | | | |
|---|---|---|---|---|
| Section | Accommodation | Food | Distance from previous facilities (km) | Cumulative (km) |
| | Sai Wan campsite | café nearby | 5.4 | 16.5 |
| | Ham Tin Wan campsite | store and café nearby | 1.9 | 18.4 |
| | | store at Tai Long (Fri–Sun only) | 1 | 19.4 |
| | YHA Bradbury Hall Youth Hostel, Chek Keng | kiosk and café in Chek Keng village, 500 metres after YHA turning | 2.1 (400 metres from trail) | 21.5 |
| 2/3 | Pak Tam Au campsite | none | 2.9 (100 metres from trail) | 24.4 |
| 3 | Cheung Sheung campsite | shop (weekends only) | 3.1 | 27.5 |
| 3/4 | Shui Long Wo campsite | shops in Sai Kung 4km away | 8.4 | 35.9 |
| 4 | Ngong Ping campsite | none | 6.2 (150 metres from trail) | 42.1 |
| 5 | | kiosk at Sha Tin Pass | 9.3 | 51.4 |
| 5/6 | | kiosk at Tai Po Road | 7 | 58.4 |
| 6/7 | | store near Shing Mun Reservoir Visitor Centre | 5.7 (1.1km from trail) | 64.1 |
| 7/8 | Lead Mine Pass campsite | none | 8.3 from previous store (80 metres from trail); 24.8km from previous campsite | 72.4 |
| 8/9 | Rotary Club campsite | Tai Mo Shan kiosk nearby | 9.2 (150 metres from trail) | 81.6 |
| | Twisk campsite | Tai Mo Shan kiosk is 500 metres away | 9.2 (100 metres from trail) | |
| 9/10 | Tin Fu Tsai campsite | none | 6.3 | 87.9 |

# DAY 1
## *Sai Kung Country Park Visitor Centre to Pak Tam Au*

| | |
|---|---|
| **Start** | Sai Kung Country Park Visitor Centre bus stop, Pak Tam Chung 西貢郊野公園遊客中心巴士站, 北潭涌 |
| **Finish** | Pak Tam Au bus stop, Pak Tam Road 北潭凹巴士站, 北潭路 |
| **Distance** | 24.5km (14.75km without Section 1) |
| **Total ascent** | 1340m (930m without Section 1) |
| **Grade** | Challenging |
| **Time** | 8hr 30min (5hr 30min without Section 1) |
| **Terrain** | Section 1 is along a quiet maintenance road; Section 2 is a mixture of stone and concrete steps, dirt and concrete paths, and some short beach segments |
| **Summits** | Sai Wan Shan (314m) |

The first section is entirely on quiet reservoir maintenance roads, despite which, surrounded in places by water and green hills, it is difficult to believe that this is in densely populated Hong Kong. The UNESCO Geopark at East Dam is well worth exploring; the optional extra leads to a natural cave, a peninsula overlooking the famous Po Pin Chau island, and a beach which backs onto natural hexagonal columns.

The second section is a long, tough yet very enjoyable walk, one of the prettiest and most popular countryside walks in Hong Kong. The views are stupendous, with the sea shimmering under a blue sky as a contrast to the calm reflective waters of High Island Reservoir. There are several fine golden-sanded beaches along the 3km-wide Tai Long Wan (大浪灣 Big Wave Bay), set against a hilly backdrop that includes the pointed Sharp Peak.

The 'Suggested itinerary' above gives various options for Day 1.

## Public transport for Day 1

**Beginning:** From Choi Hung MTR station (Kwun Tong line) exit C2, take bus 92 to Sai Kung bus terminus 西貢巴士總站, then bus 94.

**To finish at Section 1/2 junction:** Section 1 is best joined with Section 2 as there is no public transport here apart from green minibus 9A (3–6pm Sundays and public holidays only). Otherwise, use a pre-booked taxi.

**To start at Section 1/2 junction:** Get a taxi to East Dam 東壩 from Sai Kung bus terminus.

**End:** Take bus 94 to Sai Kung bus terminus, then bus 92 to Choi Hung MTR station.

**High Island Reservoir** (萬宜水庫 Million Goodness Reservoir) takes its name from High Island, which, as its name suggests, was originally an island. At a cost of HK$400 million, the island became joined to the mainland by the construction of dams to sequester fresh water. The decision to build the reservoir was spurred after mainland China cut off water supplies in the 1967 riots, when protests by pro-communists against the Hong Kong colonial government developed into violence.

*The first dam*

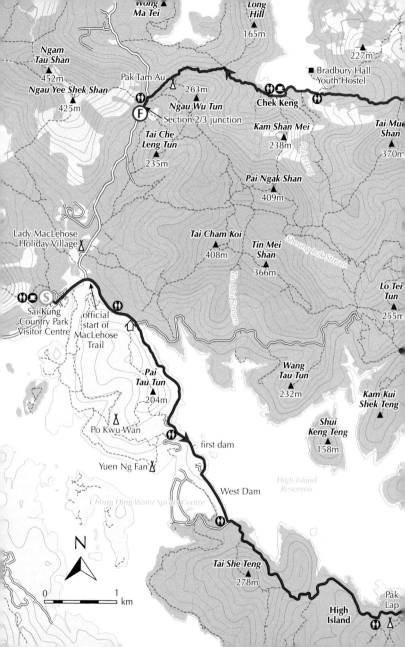

## Section 1

Go to the main road and turn left (NE). The **official start of MacLehose Trail** is about 600 metres later, immediately after a left-hand turn which you ignore. ▸ Continue straight along Tai Mong Tsai Road for 1km, then at a roundabout with a **pagoda shelter** turn right along Sai Kung Man Yee Road. Follow this maintenance road, passing the **first dam** of High Island Reservoir after 1.8km. ▸ Cross the higher **West Dam** 700 metres later, and then after another 5km cross the truly gigantic **East Dam** 東壩. This is a convenient location to end Section 1 and start Section 2.

Lady MacLehose Holiday Village is 1km along this road.

The turning for Yuen Ng Fan and Po Kwu Wan campsites is just before the first dam. The turning for Pak Lap campsite is about 1km before East Dam.

## Section 2

### Optional extra to explore the geology

This adds 4km, 175m ascent and 1hr 30min. Turn right at the north end of **East Dam**. Walk down 400 metres to the secondary **coffer dam**, built to prevent typhoons from hitting the main dam. Cross it, and at the end clamber down between the dam and the dolosse (concrete blocks) onto an unmaintained footpath. Traverse the hillside, down to a stream and along to the end of the peninsula, with great views of **Po Pin Chau**.

Retrace your steps to the beginning of the coffer dam, then turn left (W) to follow the path to

91

a sea cave, passing very close to many natural hexagonal columns. Retrace your steps to **East Dam**.

## HONG KONG UNESCO GLOBAL GEOPARK

The UNESCO Geopark contains fascinating volcanic remnants. The astounding pink hexagonal columns were discovered during the construction of East Dam. Very unusual, they originated 140 million years ago as compressed ash within a 20km-wide empty volcanic crater. As this slowly cooled, cracks propagated to form the columns.

Po Pin Chau island is composed of these same hexagonal columns. The Chinese name 破邊洲, meaning Cut in Half Island, describes its formation: firstly, a sea cave was created by erosion; this then collapsed, exposing the columns in the split.

### Main route
At the end of **East Dam**, turn left (NW) along a good foot-path signed Long Ke Village, arriving 800 metres later at the official **Section 1/2 junction**; it is halfway up the hill, for no apparent reason. Some 400 metres later, at the gate of **Wu Oi Christian Centre** 基督教互愛中心, turn right downhill following signs for Long Ke Village and Sai

*Long Ke Wan beach*

Wan. Shortly afterwards, arrive at the amazing golden sands of **Long Ke Wan beach** 浪茄灣沙灘. ▶ Walk to the other end of the beach, ford the river then ascend the steep path for 800 metres. At a **pagoda shelter**, turn left to walk along a delightful ridge, and arrive at the summit of **Sai Wan Shan** 西灣山 about 1km later.

Long Ke Wan campsite is here.

The excellent path continues; 1.7km along the route, the path splits (with no signs), but the separate paths rejoin and arrive 350 metres later at a well-made concrete crossroads in a saddle. Turn right, downhill (W), signed Sai Wan. After 1km, reach **Sai Wan** village 西灣, with restaurant, store and a beautiful double beach. Continue along the obvious path; at the end of the second beach 600 metres later, cross the bridge, signed for Ham Tin. Sai Wan campsite is on the second beach.

After 450 metres, go past **Sai Wan stargazing site**, and 1km later after a long set of steps arrive at **Ham Tin Wan beach** 鹹田灣沙灘. ▶ Follow the path signed Pak Tam Au, and veer to the left away from the beach. About 1km along this particularly wild and beautiful path, cross over a weir and arrive at a road; turn left.

Ham Tin Wan campsite is here. There is a store and café in nearby Ham Tin Wan village.

The almost deserted and partially dilapidated **Tai Long** village 大浪 is 200 metres along the road; there is a store here (open Fri–Sun only). Turn left at the end of this village to begin a long unrelenting ascent through dense woodland, then lose that altitude. ▶ After 2.5km, arrive at the mangrove-lined water's edge, with a beautiful view of Chek Keng Hau bay.

The turning for Bradbury Hall Youth Hostel is on the right about 2km from Tai Long village.

About 500 metres further, walk through the decrepit and almost totally deserted **Chek Keng** village 赤徑 (there is a kiosk and café here). At the village end, fork right. At a junction 1km later, follow the main path as it curves left, uphill (W). There is a turning for **Pak Tam Au campsite** 800 metres along. After another ascent, lasting 1.3km, reach Pak Tam Road; the **Section 2/3 junction** is 100 metres on the left. The bus stop for Sai Kung is on this side (the east side) of the road. ▶

To continue the trail, cross the road and take the steps.

# DAY 2
*Pak Tam Au to Shui Long Wo*

| | |
|---|---|
| **Start** | Pak Tam Au bus stop (note: not Pak Tam Au Management Centre), Pak Tam Road 北潭凹巴士站, 北潭路 |
| **Finish** | Shui Long Wo bus stop, Sai Sha Road 水浪窩巴士站, 西沙路 |
| **Distance** | 10.25km |
| **Total ascent** | 670m |
| **Grade** | Moderate |
| **Time** | 3hr 45min |
| **Terrain** | Begins with a long ascent via steps, followed by dirt paths; some scrambling on the optional summit |
| **Summits** | Ngau Yee Shek Shan (425m), Kai Kung Shan (399m); optional: Wa Mei Shan (391m) |

This is an incredibly rural and quiet section, with stupendous vistas, arguably some of the best of MacLehose Trail. The forests near Cheung Sheung are truly the most verdant greenery of the trail. Section 3 begins with a wonderful, if steep, ascent to a great high vantage point, followed by ridge walks and some magnificent summits. It feels like walking on top of the world, with splendid views both ahead and behind, although the best of all are from the optional extra summit at Wa Mei Shan.

Day 2 is relatively short to compensate for the challenging Day 1, or it could be joined to Section 2 if Section 1 is omitted (see 'Suggested itinerary' above).

**Public transport for Day 2**

**Beginning:** From Choi Hung MTR station (Kwun Tong line) exit C2, take bus 92 to Sai Kung bus terminus 西貢巴士總站, then bus 94.

**End:** Take bus 299X or 99 to Sai Kung bus terminus, then bus 92 to Choi Hung MTR station.

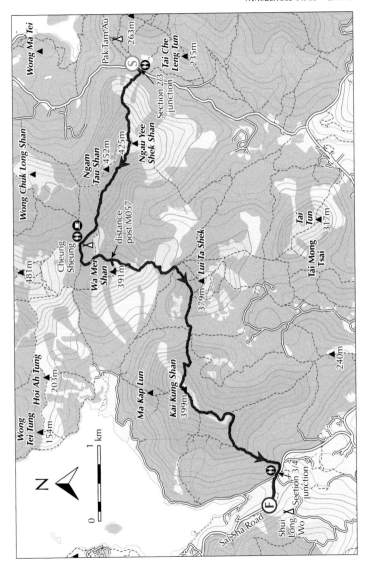

*The trail ahead has many inviting hills*

**Section 3**

Take the steps up behind the bus stop, heading W, signed Cheung Sheung. After about 1.5km of heart-thumping, lung-expanding ascent, the route levels off at **Ngau Yee Shek Shan** (牛耳石山 Cow Ear Stone Hill). Look back and admire MacLehose Section 2, plus Sharp Peak (Walk 13). Ahead are many greenswarded hills, several of which will be walked today.

Continue along a beautiful densely wooded section, with large amounts of ferns beneath, prodigious quantities of birdsong and neither sight nor sound of human existence bar the path. About 1.5km further, arrive at **Cheung Sheung campsite** 嶂上營地 (shop open at weekends only) and a multiway junction (take the first left for toilet facilities). To continue the trail, take the second left along the main path, signed Shui Long Wo. Just 250 metres thereafter, fork left (same signs), and 600 metres later arrive at MacLehose **distance post M057**. From here, there is an optional extra to Wa Mei Shan.

**Optional summit: Wa Mei Shan**
This adds 0.4km, 30m ascent and 20min. From **distance post M057**, take an unsigned, unmaintained track on the right leading up to **Wa Mei Shan** (畫眉山 Draw Eyebrow Hill, no trig point), enjoying astounding panoramic views, possibly the best of the entire MacLehose Trail. The path is slightly difficult, and could be slippery if wet; however, it is very safe and not exposed. Allow extra time to admire every peak of the eastern portion of the New Territories, a huge amount of MacLehose Trail, and much more. Retrace your steps to the trail.

When the trail emerges from the woodlands 800 metres after distance post M057, there are great views of the silver shining High Island Reservoir ahead, and behind it the big ridge at Ngau Yee Shek Shan. Continue enjoying the nature-surrounded trail for 1.6km, then at a multiway junction take the second on the right (SW), signed merely MacLehose Trail.

Follow the main trail as it contours around **Lui Ta Shek** (雷打石 Thunder Strikes Rock), followed by an unrelenting ascent, arriving at the summit of **Kai Kung Shan** (雞公山 Cockerel Peak) 1.8km after the last junction. Look backwards again to appreciate today's impressive route.

Descend along the main path for 2.4km to **Sai Sha Road**, which is the **Section 3/4 junction**. ▶ To finish today's itinerary, turn right and the bus stop is 300 metres along on this side (the north side) of the road.

To continue the trail, cross the road and take the stairs directly opposite.

# DAY 3
## *Shui Long Wo to Shek Lei Pui*

| | |
|---|---|
| **Start** | Shui Long Wo bus stop, Sai Sha Road 水浪窩巴士站, 西沙路 |
| **Finish** | Shek Lei Pui Reservoir bus stop, Tai Po Road 石梨貝水塘巴士站, 大埔公路 |
| **Distance** | 23.5km |
| **Total ascent** | 1770m |
| **Grade** | Challenging |
| **Time** | 9hr |
| **Terrain** | A mixture of stone and concrete steps, road and pavement, plus dirt, stone and concrete paths |
| **Summits** | Beacon Hill (457m); optional: Ma On Shan (702m), Lion Rock (495m) |

Today's epic route is a high-level traverse between the city of Kowloon and the New Territories, with views all the way from Hong Kong Harbour in the south to mainland China in the north. Section 4 is very varied and has one of the best ridge walks, overlooking Sai Kung and the sea. It goes through multiple types of terrain, including grasslands, scrublands and dense subtropical woodlands, ending with a view down onto the bustling centre of Kowloon. The optional ascent to Ma On Shan, the tenth highest mountain, is well worth considering.

Section 5 is almost entirely in shade through wonderful woodlands, despite being high above the surrounding countryside and city. It also has historic military relics along the route, and an optional ascent to the iconic summit of Lion Rock.

**Public transport for Day 3**

**Beginning:** From Choi Hung MTR station (Kwun Tong line) exit C2, take bus 92 to Sai Kung bus terminus 西貢巴士總站, then bus 99 or 299X.

**To finish or start at Section 4/5 junction:** There is no public transport here so it is best to link Sections 4 and 5. Otherwise, a pre-booked taxi is possible.

**End:** Take bus 81 to Prince Edward or Mong Kok MTR stations (Kwun Tong and Tsuen Wan lines).

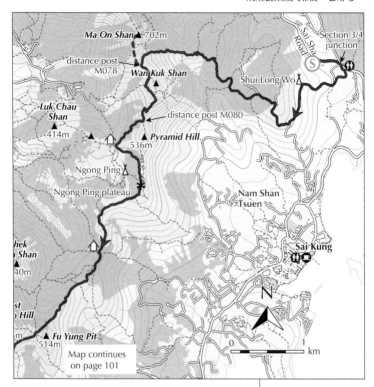

On the map: Ma On Shan ▲ 702m; distance post M078; Wan Kuk Shan ▲; Sai Sha Road; Section 3/4 junction; (S); (H); Shui Long Wo △; Luk Chau Shan ▲ 414m; distance post M080; Pyramid Hill ▲ 536m; Ngong Ping △; Ngong Ping plateau; Mau Ping Brook; Nam Shan Tsuen; Sai Kung (H); hek Shan ▲ 40m; st Hill; Fu Yung Pit ▲ 514m; Map continues on page 101; N; 0 1 km

## Section 4

From the bus stop, walk SE for 300 metres to the **Section 3/4 junction** (toilets on the left), then go right, through the picnic area for 400 metres. At a concrete road, go left uphill (SW), signed 'campsite', then almost immediately fork left at the helipad, staying on the road. **Shui Long Wo campsite** 水浪窩營地 is on the right after 400 metres.

Reach a road junction 700 metres later, go right, uphill (W), then 500 metres further turn left, downhill, at a crossroads. After 250 metres, go left off the road onto a wide dirt track signed MacLehose Trail. Walk through an incredibly dense grove of tall bamboo for 500 metres to a T-junction and turn right (unsigned, but left is to Nam Shan Tsuen). After 100 metres, go left and up the steps, now in rich subtropical woodland. A long, tough ascent of more than 300m in less than 2km leads to the highest point of Section 4 at **distance post M078**, a saddle with Ma On Shan looming impressively to the north. The diversion to the first optional summit, Ma On Shan (馬鞍山 Horse Saddle Hill), begins here.

## Optional summit: Ma On Shan
This adds 1km, 160m ascent and 40min. From **distance post M078**, turn right (not signed) and follow the path up, with some scrambling (although no danger). Pass some warning signs (which relate to a rock-climbing area beyond Ma On Shan, not to the route taken by this trail)

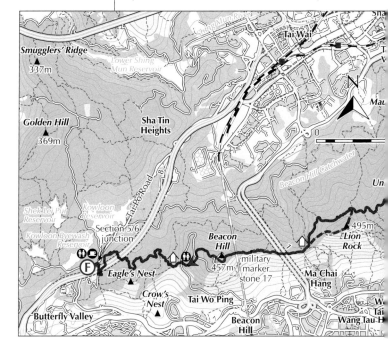

and 500 metres later reach the summit of **Ma On Shan**.
Retrace your steps to distance post M078 and turn right
(SE) to continue the trail.

Follow the obvious main path to a superb narrow ridge
walk, with great views of the New Territories to the right,
Sai Kung to the left, and Ma On Shan behind.

> The stripes of **sedimentary rocks** here are some
> of the oldest in Hong Kong, dating from the late
> Palaeozoic and Mesozoic age 400 million years
> ago. Ma On Shan peak is metamorphic limestone,
> altered by later volcanism and resistant to weather-
> ing, hence its prominence.

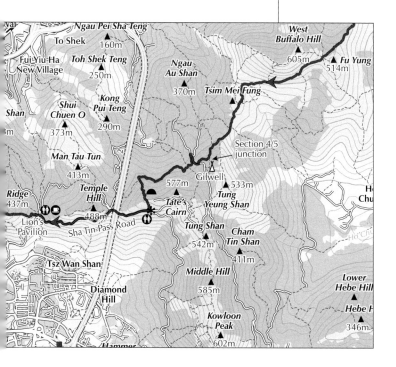

*Appreciating the MacLehose Trail route ahead: Pyramid Hill,
Tate's Cairn, Lion Rock and all the way to Tai Mo Shan*

There is a viewpoint on the far left, and a turning for Ngong Ping campsite 昂坪營地 on the right (150 metres off the trail).

After about 1km from distance post M078, and many steps down, arrive at **distance post M080**. The trail continues down, through a lovely woodland section. At a **pagoda shelter** 600 metres along, turn left following signs for Gilwell campsite, and reach the **Ngong Ping plateau** 昂坪 after 400 metres. ◄

Follow the main path for 1.6km to a footpath crossroads with a **shelter**, and go straight ahead signed Gilwell campsite. Ascend for the next 1.5km to the gap between **Buffalo Hill** and **Fu Yung Pit**, then contour for 2km (ignoring a turning for Fa Sam Hang) to a picnic area. About 500 metres after the picnic area, be careful not to miss a set of steps on the right. Descend the steps to a beautiful stream, then climb up again on the other side, followed shortly by a left-hand turn for **Gilwell campsite** 基維爾營地. ◄ This is the **Section 4/5 junction**.

Gilwell campsite is available only for large groups.

## Section 5

Along this section there are many **military marker stones**, because this used to be the frontier between British colonial Hong Kong and China, with Boundary Road the limit of the military zone. After the New Territories were acquired by Britain in

1898, this range of hills was no longer the border but the area retained military importance due to its imposing location.

From the campsite turning, head SW for 200 metres to a road and turn right, downhill, signed Tate's Cairn. At a crossroads after 200 metres, turn left onto a dirt track. At the second military marker stone 1km along, follow the main path as it veers left (SE). Continue for 400 metres, pass a World War 2 trench, and reach a large stone-built structure; turn left onto a concrete road.

Look out for a **cave** excavated by the Japanese in World War 2 to hide soldiers and ambush the British if they retook Hong Kong. The cave is one of several built throughout Hong Kong, but the Japanese had surrendered before they were ever used.

Go immediately right and follow the trail S for 150 metres to the bottom of a set of steps; turn right (W) onto **Sha Tin Pass Road** 沙田坳道 (which is also Wilson Trail). Continue along this road for nearly 3km to reach **Lion's Pavilion** 獅子亭. ▶ Shortly after, at a leftward hairpin bend, go up steps on the right-hand side of the road, heading W into Lion Rock Country Park, signed Lion Rock. The top of the steps 500 metres later marks the beginning of **Unicorn Ridge** (雞胸山 Chicken Breast Hill, which has no actual peak).

There are toilets and a kiosk here.

*There is plenty of shade along Unicorn Ridge*

103

Walk along in light subtropical woodland with some shade, past more military marker stones, for just over 1km, to reach a turning on the left for **Lion Rock** 獅子山. A diversion to Lion Rock leaves the route here.

### Optional summit: Lion Rock

This adds 120m ascent and 30min, but the distance is the same as if you stay on the main trail. Take the turning to the left. Arrive at Lion Rock 獅子山 summit (rump) after a long set of steps (about 350 metres), then turn right to walk W along the ridge, passing Lion Rock (body). Continue along the path and go down the steps just before Lion Rock (head). ◄ Rejoin MacLehose Trail after 400 metres.

*Beware: fatalities have occurred on the climb to Lion Rock (head), so it is not included in this route.*

If you are not detouring to Lion Rock, continue along the trail, past more military marker stones and some ruinous pillboxes (part of Gin Drinkers Line).

## THE GIN DRINKERS LINE

The Gin Drinkers Line ran for 18km from what used to be Gin Drinkers Bay, on the east of Kowloon (now subsumed by land reclamation), to Sai Kung via Shing Mun, Lion Rock and all points between. A defensive line built by the British between World War 1 and 2, it was supposed to hold off a Japanese attack for six months, yet lasted only two days.

Arrive at a multiway junction with a **shelter** after 1km. ◄ Go straight ahead (SW) signed Beacon Hill (no MacLehose signs). Go past more evidence of Hong Kong's military past, and arrive at **military marker stone 17** after 800 metres. There are multiple paths here, but go straight ahead (W) up the steps (no sign). Cross over a concrete road 600 metres later, go straight ahead and curve right around the perimeter wall of the subsidiary radar dome atop **Beacon Hill** 畢架山. ◄

*The diversion to Lion Rock summit rejoins 150 metres before this shelter.*

*The huge main radar dome is hidden from view.*

After a trig point, go down the steps and 400 metres later cross straight over Lung Yan Road. Cross over the same road again 300 metres further on, reaching a T-junction by a **shelter** after 150 metres. Go right (NW);

shortly thereafter, at the bottom of a set of short steps, go left at another T-junction. This is a very enjoyable section through wonderful dense subtropical woodland with huge amounts of birdsong and Shiuying bamboo. ▸

At a stream 2km along, go right (downstream) to Piper's Hill Road, then go right, downhill (no signs) for 150 metres to the major **Tai Po Road**, which is the **Section 5/6 junction**. Go left to reach the bus stop. ▸

Shiuying bamboo is Hong Kong's endemic species, only discovered in 1981.

To continue the trail, walk across the road via a footbridge, where there is a kiosk.

# DAY 4

*Shek Lei Pui Reservoir to Route Twisk*

| | |
|---|---|
| **Start** | Shek Lei Pui Reservoir bus stop, Tai Po Road 石梨貝水塘巴士站, 大埔公路 |
| **Finish** | Tai Mo Shan Country Park bus stop, Route Twisk 大帽山郊野公園巴士站, 荃錦公路 |
| **Distance** | 20.75km |
| **Total ascent** | 1680m |
| **Grade** | Challenging |
| **Time** | 8hr 15min |
| **Terrain** | Along quiet maintenance roads at the beginning and end, with mainly dirt paths in between |
| **Summits** | Needle Hill (532m), Grassy Hill (647m), Sze Fong Shan (784m), Tai Mo Shan (957m); optional: Miu Ko Toi (767m) |

Section 6 begins by a cluster of attractive reservoirs with a large monkey population. Easy walking along a quiet maintenance road is followed by a good path on Smugglers' Ridge, with both fascinating military relics and excellent views of the path ahead, including today's summits.

Section 7 includes exhilarating ascents of Needle Hill and Grassy Hill, rewarded by fantastic panoramic views. The first part of Section 8 is a delight, ascending the highest peak in Hong Kong, Tai Mo Shan, among swathes of Chinese silvergrass. The descent on the road is slightly monotonous but easy walking, ending along a quiet, green section.

## Public transport for Day 4

**Beginning:** From Prince Edward MTR station (Tsuen Wan and Kwun Tong lines) exit E, head N along Nathan Road for 50 metres and take bus 81.

**To finish at Section 6/7 junction:** Turn left (W) down the road signed 'maxi-cab' and follow it for just over 1km to Shing Mun Country Park Visitor Centre (with a kiosk). Take green minibus 82 to the terminus on Shiu Wo Street, then go NE down an alleyway (signed MTR). Turn right at its end, go up an escalator and cross two roads via a pedestrian walkway leading to Tsuen Wan MTR station (Tsuen Wan line) 荃灣港鐵站.

**To start at Section 6/7 junction:** From Tsuen Wan MTR station (Tsuen Wan line) exit B1, cross two roads via a pedestrian bridge, turn right, descend to Castle Peak Road, then take the first left down an alleyway to Shiu Wo Street; the minibus stop is to the left. Take green minibus 82 to the terminus at Shing Mun Reservoir 城門水塘. Walk SW up the road (away from Shing Mun Country Park Visitor Centre) to reach the Section 6/7 junction in just over 1km.

**To finish or start at Section 7/8 junction:** There is no public transport here so it is easier to join Sections 7 and 8. However, it is possible to finish here by following Section 7 of Wilson Trail to San Uk Ka minibus stop (2.5km) and taking green minibus 23S or 23K to Tai Po Market MTR station (East Rail line). To start here, reverse the above.

**End:** Take bus 51 (hourly on weekdays, every 15min at weekends) to Tsuen Wan MTR station (Tsuen Wan line) 荃灣港鐵站.

### Section 6

Head uphill (NE) for 150 metres, then take the first left onto Golden Hill Road into Kam Shan Country Park (ignore confusing MacLehose signs here, pointing in different directions). ◀ Cross the dams and continue along the road for 2.5km (not turning off onto Wilson Trail). Just before a **shelter**, go right up the steps onto **Smugglers' Ridge**, signed Shing Mun Reservoir. About 900 metres along, get to the first of several tunnel entrances at **Shing Mun Redoubt**.

**Shing Mun Redoubt** is a defensive structure, part of the Gin Drinkers Line (described in Section 5).

The Kowloon Reservoirs hold nearly 3 billion litres of fresh water, enough to last Hong Kong for just one day!

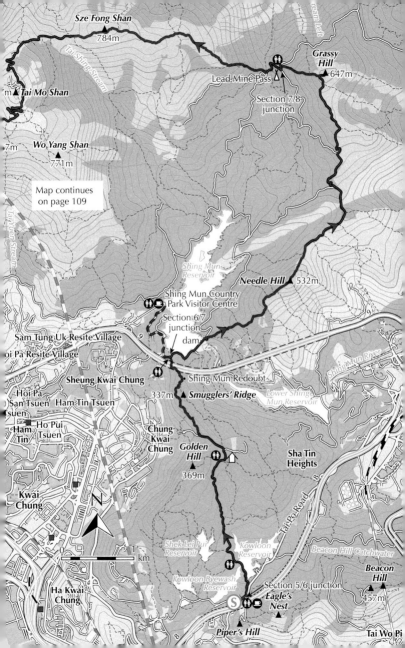

Sze Fong Shan
784m

m ▲Tai Mo Shan

7m

Wo Yang Shan
771m

Tai Shing Stream

Grassy Hill
647m

Lead Mine Pass

Section 7/8
junction

Map continues
on page 109

Tai Yuen Stream

Shing Mun
Reservoir

Needle Hill ▲ 532m

Shing Mun Country
Park Visitor Centre

Section 6/7
junction
dam

Sam Tung Uk Resite Village
oi Pa Resite Village

Sheung Kwai Chung

Hoi Pa
San Tsuen
Tsuen

Ham Tin Tsuen

Ham
Tin

Ho Pui
Tsuen

Chung
Kwai
Chung

Shing Mun Redoubt

337m    ▲ Smugglers' Ridge

Lower Shing
Mun Reservoir

Shing Mun River

Kwai
Chung

Golden
Hill
369m

Sha Tin
Heights

Tai Po Road

N

0                    1
km

Shek Lei Pui
Reservoir

Kowloon
Byewash Reservoir

Kowloon
Reservoir

Beacon Hill Catchwater

Ha Kwai
Chung

Section 5/6 junction

S    Eagle's
Nest

Beacon
Hill
457m

Piper's Hill

Tai Wo P

Underground there are many tunnels named after London roads, such as Charing Cross and Shaftesbury Avenue.

After 450 metres, arrive at Shing Mun barbecue area (with toilets); this is the **Section 6/7 junction**.

### Section 7

Head E along the maintenance road and arrive at the main **dam** after 400 metres. ◄ Cross over the dam (which is also Wilson Trail), following the road as it curves up and right for just 100 metres, then turn right, up the steps. A long and enjoyable ascent of nearly 2km leads to the summit of **Needle Hill** 針山, where the views seem to encompass the whole of Hong Kong territory. From here, Hong Kong's tallest building, the 484m International Commerce Centre, looks impossibly tall.

Continue along for 500 metres to a concrete road. Follow it for 1km, initially on very open terrain progressing to lovely shaded subtropical woodland, to a fork. Go right (NW), uphill, signed Grassy Hill and Lead Mine Pass. At the next fork 500 metres later, go right, signed Grassy Hill (not left to Lead Mine Pass).

*Shing Mun, meaning Fort Gate, is the name of a Ming Dynasty military base. The area is locally known as Monkey Hill because of the resident monkey population.*

*Shing Mun Reservoir with Tai Mo Shan behind*

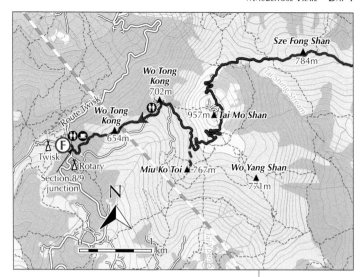

Nearly at the top, 1.3km along, are slightly confusing signs, both saying MacLehose, one left and one right. Go right to the summit of **Grassy Hill** 草山 (Hong Kong's 14th highest), then retrace your steps to the confusing signs. Now take the other turning, a downward dirt path bearing W towards Tai Mo Shan. At the bottom of the steps 700 metres along, turn left, downhill onto a concrete road (no sign). Shortly after, take the first right, downhill, signed Shing Mun Reservoir and Campsite. Walk down, past a helipad, and 400 metres later is Lead Mine Pass, the **Section 7/8 junction**. ▶

Lead Mine Pass campsite is 80 metres down the road.

## Section 8

Head NW up to the MacLehose Section 8 gate, and turn right after 400 metres. ▶ This is the quietest section of the entire trail, progressing through beautiful woodland into open grassland for 2.2km to **Sze Fong Shan** 四方山.

Minimal signage; don't go to Chuen Lung.

**Sze Fong Shan** (meaning Square Hill) is Hong Kong's fourth highest mountain. It is one of the few

*Grassland near Sze Fong Shan, with the famous Miscanthus sinensis*

places in Hong Kong to possibly spot a Chinese francolin (it belongs to the quail family but is three to four times bigger).

Continue for another 700 metres to reach a concrete road. Follow it, signed Route Twisk, for about 1km to a road junction; go left and uphill. Reach another road junction after 700 metres; this is as close to the summit of **Tai Mo Shan** as is possible.

## TAI MO SHAN

Hong Kong's highest mountain, Tai Mo Shan 大帽山, is named Big Hat Hill for its shape. Its Chinese name sounds like Big Fog Hill and is widely used by Hongkongers as it aptly describes the misty mountaintop. It is festooned with radar and broadcasting equipment, protected by vicious razor wire.

Turn left at this junction and then simply follow the tarmac road as it zigzags down the mountain. A turning to Miu Ko Toi, an optional extra for summit baggers, is 1.7km down the road.

**Optional summit: Miu Ko Toi**

This adds 0.8km, 30m ascent and 15min. By a 'no camping, no fire' sign, 1.7km after Tai Mo Shan, turn left from the road onto a dirt track and follow it for 400 metres to the unmarked summit of **Miu Ko Toi** 妙高台, Hong Kong's seventh highest peak. Retrace your steps to the road.

About 1.8km from the Miu Ko Toi turning, reach a T-junction (with barrier to stop cars). Turn right, signed Route Twisk, then almost immediately take a footpath left off the road. Follow this back to the same road after 250 metres, then take a footpath on the right. After another 1.3km arrive at Tai Mo Shan Country Park Visitor Centre; take the steps to the right of it, leading after 200 metres to the bus stop on Route Twisk, which is the **Section 8/9 junction**. ▶

There are two campsites and a kiosk nearby.

The road **Route Twisk** is not eponymous, but is named after the initials of the two places it links: Tsuen Wan and Shek Kong. Where did the 'i' come from? Allegedly, it was a misprint of 'Route TW/SK' in a construction project document.

# DAY 5

*Route Twisk to Tuen Mun*

| | |
|---|---|
| **Start** | Tai Mo Shan Country Park bus stop, Route Twisk 大帽山郊野公園巴士站, 荃錦公路 |
| **Finish** | Tuen Mun MTR station (Tuen Ma line) 屯門港鐵站 |
| **Distance** | 22.5km |
| **Total ascent** | 990m |
| **Grade** | Difficult |
| **Time** | 6hr 30min |
| **Terrain** | Much is on quiet maintenance road, with some dirt path and a long section by a catchwater |

Section 9 is entirely on quiet maintenance roads through impressive mature subtropical woodland, the least exciting section but easy walking. Section 10 walks through the area around Tai Lam Chung Reservoir, taking in the beautiful Reservoir Islands Viewpoint and some temples. It finishes with restful walking along a catchwater to complete the entire MacLehose Trail.

**Public transport for Day 5**

**Beginning:** From Tsuen Wan MTR station (Tsuen Wan line) exit A, turn left up the first set of stairs to a bus stop (don't go to the bus terminus). Take bus 51 (direction Sheung Tsuen).

**To finish or start at Section 9/10 junction:** To start or finish here is difficult because there is no public transport and no road, hence Section 9 is best joined with Section 10.

**Section 9**

The Twisk campsite 荃錦營地 is 500 metres along, with toilets.

From the bus stop, walk down the road to the entrance to Tai Lam Country Park Twisk Management Centre. Turn into it, heading NW, and continue along the road through the management centre. ◄

Simply stay on the maintenance road (which is also the Twisk Mountain Bike Trail) for about 2km, then fork right, by some **toilets**, signed Tai Lam Chung Reservoir and Tin Fu Tsai. At the picnic site by Tin Fu Tsai Mountain Bike Trail 2.3km later, fork left (same signs). About 750 metres later, by a **shelter**, go right at a T-junction (same signs). Just over 1km along, **Tin Fu Tsai campsite 田夫仔營地** is on the left, which is the **Section 9/10 junction**.

**Section 10**

Continue straight on (W) along the road, now following signs for Tai Lam Chung Reservoir (and ignoring signs for Tin Fu Tsai 600 metres later, which is to the village only). Reach a road after 2.5km, turn left, then immediately fork right to head SW. There are multiple signs here; follow the sign for Tai Tong Shan Road.

Continue along the road for 2 km. ▶ Be careful not to miss the left-hand turn (minimal signage for MacLehose) by some **toilets**, signed Tai Tong Valley and Reservoir Islands Viewpoint. Pass a **temple** 350 metres later.

These tiny **temples**, dedicated to Heavenly Generals and Earth God, are often found on ancient ways between villages, to protect travellers and guard the area from evil.

Finally leaving the concrete road at its end 400 metres along, progress onto a narrow footpath, now signed Wong Nai Tung Reservoir and Reservoir Islands Viewpoint. At a second **temple** after 200 metres, go straight on at the junction, following the same signs. Some 800 metres along, on the left, there is a worthwhile there-and-back excursion to **Reservoir Islands Viewpoint**.

**Reservoir Islands Viewpoint** (千島湖清景台 Thousand Islands Lake Viewpoint) is 200 metres from the trail. It provides a fascinating otherworldly vista of myriads of irregularly scalloped emerald islands nestled in sparkling green water.

From the picnic area at the top of Tai Lam Chung Reservoir, the route is lined with sweet gum (*Liquidambar formosana*), which turns a delightful shade of red in autumn/winter.

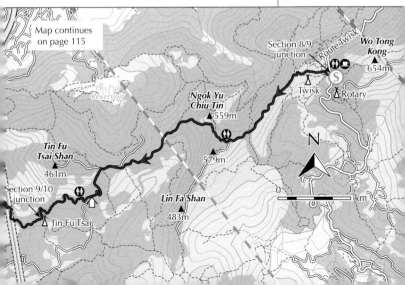

*Thousand Islands Lake*

Por Lo Shan ▲

Tuen Mun San Hui

official end of MacLehose Trail

Tuen Mun Kau Hui

Ⓕ

Pui To light rail station

Tuen Mun

Kau Keng Shan ▲ 507m

Castle Peak Bay

Tai Lam Chung Catchwater

So Kwun Wat

About 1km after the turning for the viewpoint, arrive at a quiet maintenance road and go left, downhill, signed MacLehose 10. Walk along this peaceful, shaded road, passing (but not crossing) a small subsidiary **dam** 1.5km along. After a further 600 metres, turn right at a road barrier. Reach **Tai Lam Chung Catchwater** 大欖涌引水道 200 metres later, and turn left to follow it (SW).

## CATCHWATERS

A significant portion of this section is along catchwaters, rainwater drainage channels, which are part of a massive civil engineering project of slope management. Between the end of World War 2 and the 1970s, 470 people died in landslides in Hong Kong, triggered by tropical rainstorms. Starting in 1977, every slope in the vicinity of inhabited areas or infrastructure has been regularly inspected and, where necessary, actively managed to prevent such calamity. This has led to a reduction in deaths caused by landslides from a peak of 140 per year in 1972 to effectively zero.

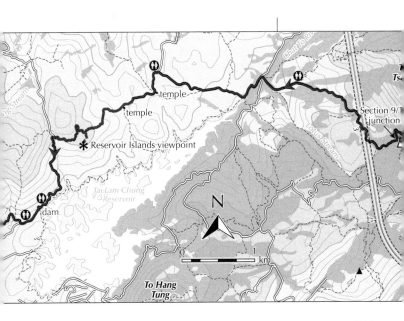

*The end of MacLehose Trail*

Walk along this catchwater as it follows the contour line around **Kau Keng Shan** for about 6km, in places lined with orchid trees. Immediately before the track alongside the catchwater becomes some upward steps, turn left, signed MacLehose 10. Just 20 metres later, go down the steps on the left. Follow this path downhill (ignoring any option that doesn't go downwards) for 500 metres to Castle Peak Road and the **official end of MacLehose Trail** at distance marker 200.

The **orchid tree** (*Bauhinia blakeana*, named after Sir Henry Blake, Governor of Hong Kong 1898–1903) flowers from November to March. All orchid trees are clones from a sterile hybrid discovered by a French botanist who was hiking in the territory. The orchid tree became Hong Kong's emblem in 1965.

To get to public transport, turn left then immediate right, walk across the road and onto a pedestrian bridge. Reach **Pui To light rail station** 杯渡輕鐵站 in less than 100 metres, go through it and down the steps at the other end. Continue straight ahead for 400 metres, cross another road to arrive at **Tuen Mun MTR station**.

# TREK 4
## *Wilson Trail*

| | |
|---|---|
| **Start** | Wilson Trail bus stop, Stanley Gap Road, Stanley 衛奕信徑巴士站, 赤柱峽道, 赤柱 |
| **Finish** | Nam Chung Lee Uk village bus stop, Luk Keng Road 南涌李屋村巴士站, 鹿頸路 |
| **Distance** | 80.25km |
| **Total ascent** | 5420m |
| **Time** | 5 days (30hr 15min) |
| **Terrain** | All on excellent paths, a mixture of stone and dirt, plus a small amount of very quiet road; many steps, also forested sections, and ending with a superb ridge walk |
| **Map** | Sections 1 and 2: Hong Kong Island & Neighbouring Islands; Sections 3–5: Sai Kung & Clear Water Bay; Sections 6–10: North East & Central New Territories |

Wilson Trail is named after Sir David Wilson, Governor of Hong Kong 1987–92. Opened in 1996, it traverses the whole of Hong Kong from south to north via eight of the country parks, with minimal urban walking. As each section has its own character, it offers an appealing romp through the territory.

The first two sections go through hilly and relatively undeveloped areas of Hong Kong Island, with views metamorphosing from sea to skyscrapers. Unusually for a long-distance trail, it uses public transport to cross Hong Kong Harbour from Section 2 to 3. The middle sections travel through old villages via green and shaded paths around some of the many reservoirs. The final two sections end in the most remote area, bordering mainland China, and encompass the finest ridge walk of the region at Pat Sin Leng. These are the toughest but also the most rewarding sections of the entire trail.

### Suggested itinerary
The entire trail can be walked according to our suggested itinerary below, or tailored to your own personal

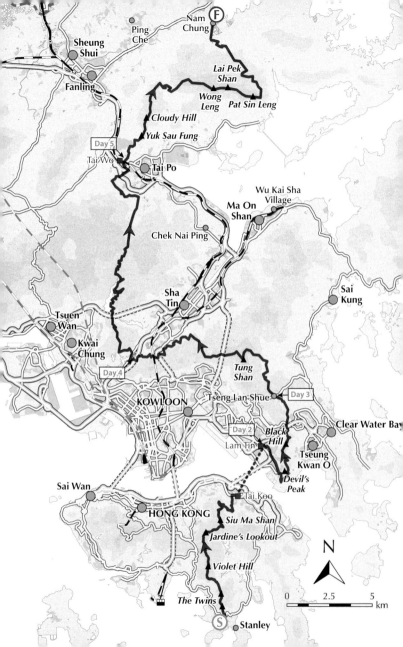

Nam Chung

Ping Che

Sheung Shui

Fanling

*Lai Pek Shan*

*Wong Leng*

*Pat Sin Leng*

*Cloudy Hill*

*Yuk Sau Fung*

Day 5

Tai Wo

Tai Po

Wu Kai Sha Village

Ma On Shan

Chek Nai Ping

Sha Tin

Sai Kung

Tsuen Wan

Kwai Chung

Day 4

*Tung Shan*

KOWLOON

Tseng Lan Shue

Day 3

Day 2

Lam Tin

*Black Hill*

Clear Water Ba

Tseung Kwan O

Sai Wan

*Devil's Peak*

Tai Koo

HONG KONG

*Siu Ma Shan*

*Jardine's Lookout*

*Violet Hill*

*The Twins*

S  Stanley

N

0   2.5   5
km

preference, stamina and pace of walking. If you are feeling superhuman, it is possible, although exhausting, to add the relatively short Day 2 (Section 3 alone) to either Day 1 or Day 3. This would shorten the hike to four days, which would include one very long, tough day. Each day in the itinerary can be treated as a day walk. The Pat Sin Leng ridge walk (Section 9) is arguably Hong Kong's best ridge walk, so if you don't want to miss it but are unable to complete the entire Day 5 itinerary, an alternative, shorter version is suggested, omitting the second part of Section 8 and Section 10.

Accommodation is not available along the trail, apart from campsites in Sections 7 and 9. With Hong Kong's superb transport system, it is easier to return to a fixed base after each day's walking. The optimum base for this trail would be anywhere in central Kowloon near an MTR station.

In the following table:

*   The figures for **each individual section** include the trail itself plus transit to and from public transport at the beginning and end of the section.

*Stanley in the silvery early morning light as seen from the steep ascent (Day 1)*

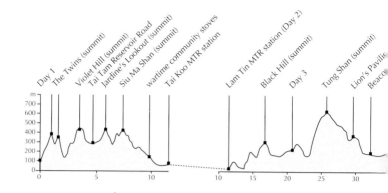

- **Each daily total** includes transit to and from public transport at the beginning and end of the day (but does not include transit for intervening sections).
- The **overall grade for each day** takes into account cumulative distance and ascent (so although each individual section may be easy if done on its own, when combined with other sections the difficulty is likely to increase).

| Stage | Sections | Distance | Ascent | Time | Grade | Note |
|---|---|---|---|---|---|---|
| Day 1 | 1 | 5.3km | 630m | 2hr 30min | moderate | |
| | 2 | 7.3km | 490m | 2hr 30min | easy | |
| | **Total** | **11.5km** | **1040m** | **5hr** | **difficult** | |
| Day 2 | 3 | **9.25km** | **560m** | **3hr 30min** | moderate | |
| Day 3 | 4 | 8km | 680m | 3hr | moderate | no transport at section end |
| | 5 | 8km | 590m | 3hr | easy | no transport at section start |
| | **Total** | **16km** | **1270m** | **6hr** | **difficult** | |
| Day 4 | 6 | 6.8km | 410m | 2hr | easy | |
| | 7 | 12.2km | 600m | 4hr | easy | no transport at section end |

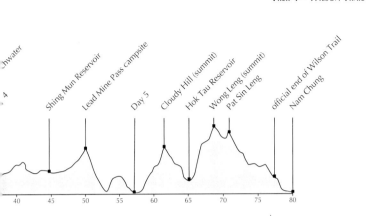

| Stage | Sections | Distance | Ascent | Time | Grade | Note |
|-------|----------|----------|--------|------|-------|------|
| | 8 (1st part) | 4.4km | 200m | 1hr 30min | easy | no transport at section start |
| | **Total** | **20.5km** | **1080m** | **6hr 45min** | **difficult** | |
| Day 5 | 8 (2nd part) | 4.5km | 490m | 2hr | moderate | no transport at section end |
| | 9 | 10.5km | 800m | 4hr 30min | difficult | no transport at section start or end |
| | 10 | 8km | 180m | 2hr 30min | easy | no transport at section start |
| | **Total** | **23km** | **1470m** | **9hr** | **challenging** | |

# DAY 1
## *Stanley Gap Road to Tai Koo*

| | |
|---|---|
| **Start** | Wilson Trail bus stop, Stanley Gap Road, Stanley 衛奕信徑巴士站, 赤柱峽道, 赤柱 |
| **Finish** | Tai Koo MTR station (Island line) 太古港鐵站 |
| **Distance** | 11.5km |
| **Total ascent** | 1040m |
| **Grade** | Difficult |
| **Time** | 5hr |
| **Terrain** | Many stone and concrete steps, with some dirt paths, and a small amount of road at the end |
| **Summits** | The Twins (386m and 363m), Violet Hill (433m), Jardine's Lookout (433m), Siu Ma Shan (424m) |

This is a tough but exhilarating beginning to the trail, traversing the entirety of Hong Kong Island from south to north, with an impressive gain in altitude followed by an equally significant descent. The views are ample reward, metamorphosing from open sea views to the shining skyscraper-adorned heart of the territory. Along the way, the trail encompasses four summits and a lot of steps. It ends at an MTR station for a convenient transfer to the mainland.

### Public transport for Day 1

**Beginning:** From Hong Kong MTR station (Tung Chung line) exit B1, take bus 6 from the bus terminus across the road to the right.

**To finish at Section 1/2 junction:** Turn left at Tai Tam Reservoir Road. At the end of the road 250 metres later is the junction with Wong Nai Chung Gap Road. Tai Tam Reservoir Road bus stop is on the opposite side of that road. Take bus 6 or 66 to Central Exchange Square for Hong Kong MTR station (Tung Chung line).

**To start at Section 1/2 junction:** From Hong Kong MTR station (Tung Chung line) exit B1, cross the road and the bus station is to the right. Take bus 6 to

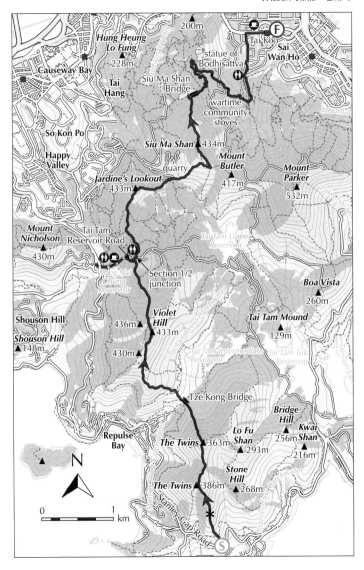

Wong Nai Chung Reservoir Park bus stop, Wong Nai Chung Gap Road 黃泥涌水塘公園巴士站, 黃泥涌峽道. Take the first set of steps on the left immediately after a garage, go up to Tai Tam Reservoir Road and turn left. Walk for 500 metres, passing Wong Nai Chung Reservoir, and the Wilson Trail gate marking the Section 1/2 junction is on the left.

## Section 1

From the bus stop, go up the very obvious steps adjacent to the Wilson Trail plaque and signboard, following signs for **Ma Kong Shan View Compass**. Ascend 300m over 1km, going across Stanley West Catchwater and past Ma Kong Shan View Compass, and eventually arrive at the summit of the **first of The Twins**.

> **The Twins** are also called Ma Kong Shan 孖崗山, meaning Twin Peaks Hill. The rewards for this climb are the amazing views of many boats dotted on the silver shining seas, Dragon's Back (Hong Kong Trail) and Lamma Island (Walks 19 and 20).

After the **second of The Twins** 500 metres later, descend to **Tze Kong Bridge** 紫崗橋 across Stanley West Catchwater. Ignore paths both left and right, and ascend again for another 1.4km to one of the three summits of **Violet Hill** 紫羅蘭山 (Walk 17). ◄ At a T-junction 150 metres later, go right, signed Hong Kong Parkview, and descend for 1km to **Tai Tam Reservoir Road**. To continue the trail, turn right and take the second footpath on the left 100 metres later, where a large gate for both Wilson and Hong Kong Trails marks the **Section 1/2 junction**.

The view has now changed from panoramic sea views in the south to the impressive skyscraper-filled Hong Kong central area ahead.

## Section 2

Go through the gate (which marks the start point for Wilson Trail, Section 2, and Hong Kong Trail, Section 5). Turn immediate right up the steps following signs for Jardine's Lookout. Go past Osborn Memorial and after 1km arrive at **Jardine's Lookout** 渣甸山.

Named after William Jardine, founder of Jardine Matheson import–export company, **Jardine's Lookout** was used in the 19th century as an observation point. From here, the company could keep watch for its own ships and arrange to be waiting for them as they docked, thus receiving news ahead of its competitors. Today, it is a spectacular vantage point for walkers, with panoramic views over the heart of the city and the whole expanse of Hong Kong Harbour.

Next, follow signs for Mount Butler (although the route does not go there) and cross Jardine North catchwater 600 metres later, with a **quarry** on the left and the cluster of **Tai Tam Reservoirs** on the far right. Ignoring other paths, take a left-hand turn up the steps 500 metres after the quarry, signed Wilson Trail. After 400 metres, arrive at the summit of **Siu Ma Shan** (小馬山 Little Horse Hill).

Descend for 750 metres, cross **Siu Ma Shan Bridge** 小馬山橋 and arrive at a T-junction. Turn right, downhill, signed Sir Cecil's Ride. ▶ At the bottom of the steps 300 metres later, turn left at a T-junction with a dirt track, following signs for Braemar Hill. After 600 metres, go right at a crossroads, again following Sir Cecil's Ride for another 200 metres. Fork right down the steps, now following signs for Mount Parker Road.

Pass a shrine on the left, then at the bottom of the stairs is a crossroads with a **statue of Bodhisattva** (holding

Sir Cecil Clementi, Governor of Hong Kong 1925–35, was fluent in Cantonese, which was unusual for those times. He and his wife rode these trails regularly.

*Wartime community stoves*

125

a baby). Turn right (S), signed Wilson Trail, to Kornhill. Reach a tarmac road after 200 metres, turn left then almost immediately right down steps, following signs for Quarry Bay Tree Walk and Kornhill. Just 200 metres along, arrive at some **wartime community stoves** (built during World War 2 but never used), followed by a second group 200 metres later. Turn left following the same signs and continue on the main path for 850 metres.

Turn left onto Greig Road, following signs for Tai Koo MTR, and arrive at King's Road after 350 metres. Turn right and **Tai Koo MTR station** is 300 metres along. This is the end of Section 2, although there is no sign. ◂

*To continue the trail, take the MTR to the beginning of Section 3.*

# DAY 2
## *Lam Tin to Tseng Lan Shue*

| | |
|---|---|
| **Start** | Lam Tin MTR station (Kwun Tong line) 藍田港鐵站 |
| **Finish** | Tseng Lan Shue bus stop, Clear Water Bay Road 井欄樹巴士站, 清水灣道 |
| **Distance** | 9.25km |
| **Total ascent** | 560m |
| **Grade** | Moderate |
| **Time** | 3hr 30min |
| **Terrain** | A mixture of steps, pavement, dirt and concrete paths |
| **Summits** | Devil's Peak (222m), unnamed peak (281m), Black Hill (304m) |

Day 2 (Section 3 alone) is relatively short, a well-deserved easier day after a tough Day 1. Suitable for families, this starts urban yet has some lovely hills and peaks. It begins at an MTR station, a convenient start place with no bus transfer. It also includes historical interest, some quaint villages, subtropical woodland and a beautiful river section. Note that there are no signs in the urban portion at the beginning, and only intermittently throughout.

**Public transport for Day 2**

**End:** Take bus 91 or 92 to Choi Hung or Diamond Hill MTR stations (Kwun Tong line).

### Section 3

From the MTR station exit A, turn right onto Kai Tin Road, heading S. At the end of the road 400 metres later, turn left onto Lei Yue Mun Road. Walk along for about 1km to the end, turn left at the roundabout onto Ko Chiu Road, then take the second turning on the right, signed Chinese Permanent Cemetery (no road name).

Continue uphill for 600 metres and shortly after the second **shelter** turn left up the steps, with the first sign for Wilson Trail. At the top of the steps, go left, upwards, signed Devil's Peak. There are two excursions here: a right-hand turn after 200 metres for Gough Battery (signed Devil's Peak Fortification) and a left-hand turn shortly afterwards for Devil's Peak Redoubt.

*Returning to the route from Devil's Peak gives great views of Hong Kong Island*

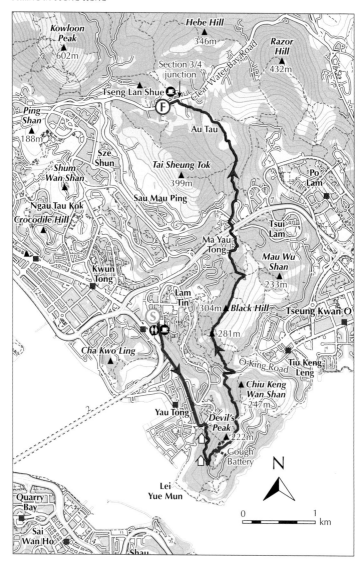

**Gough Battery**, built in 1898 and probably named after the Commander-in-Chief of British forces in China, Viscount Gough, used to be armed with enormous 23cm-calibre naval guns. More interestingly, nature has almost reclaimed this military remnant, peace replacing war. (This excursion adds 200 metres return; after visiting, retrace your steps to the main trail.)

**Devil's Peak** is allegedly named after the appallingly bloodthirsty Cheng Lin Cheong, a pirate in the pre-British period. In colonial times, it was transformed into Devil's Peak Redoubt in 1914, hence the Chinese name Pau Toi Shan 炮台山, meaning Cannon Peak. The British guns were guarding the entrance to Hong Kong Harbour, but after an intense battle in World War 2, the Japanese forces set up artillery here, pounding Hong Kong into submission. (This excursion adds 500 metres return; after exploring the ruins, retrace your steps to the main trail.)

Reach a junction 30 metres after the Devil's Peak turning, turn left and continue for 500 metres, ignoring a left turn that goes back to Devil's Peak. Arrive at a T-junction, turn right and continue for 700 metres. There are some confusing signs here, showing Wilson Trail straight ahead as well as up steps to the right; this is because the trail was diverted due to a landslide. Take either, as they both lead to the same place.

After about 300 metres, go down some steps on the left leading to **O King Road** 澳景路. Turn right, then 150 metres later turn left up the steps. At a shelter 100 metres later, turn right down the steps to arrive at a multiway junction. Go straight ahead up the steps, signed Wilson Trail. Follow the main path upwards for 500 metres to an **unnamed peak** (281m) with a trig point. Go straight past it, heading NE along the ridge, following the main path for 400 metres past a shelter and two intriguing giant plain white boards. This leads to this section's highest point, **Black Hill** 五桂山 (no trig point).

What are the **two giant white boards**? At first glance they appear to have no function; they are not solar panels nor are they for advertising. In fact they are former aviation reflectors from the time when Hong Kong Airport was in Kowloon. For night operations, these would have passively reflected the lights of the aircraft.

Follow the path as it enters subtropical woodland, and 500 metres later turn left following steps downhill signed Wilson Trail. At the bottom of the steps, reach a concrete path and go right following signs for Wilson Trail and Ma Yau Tong 馬遊塘. After 300 metres, reach **Ma Yau Tong** village and turn right at a T-junction. Follow the route for 500 metres to a crossroads (with Po Lam Road), and go straight across at the traffic lights.

Walk along Tsui Lam Road for 300 metres, then turn left onto another road signed for Au Tau 凹頭. After 1km, arrive at **Au Tau** village. ◀ At the end of the road, go up a set of steps behind some houses, heading N (no signs, but there are signs later). The trail goes past many pretty smallholdings, through subtropical woodland by a beautiful river and a water channel, and 750 metres later reaches a road. Continue to follow the footpath, now alongside a catchwater, and arrive at Clear Water Bay Road. This is the **Section 3/4 junction**. To complete today's itinerary, go left for 200 metres to Tseng Lan Shue bus stop (on the south side of the road). ◀

The chains across the road are to stop cars, not walkers.

To continue to Section 4, cross the road using the underpass.

# DAY 3

*Tseng Lan Shue to Kowloon Reservoir*

| | |
|---|---|
| **Start** | Tseng Lan Shue bus stop, Clear Water Bay Road 井欄樹巴士站, 清水灣道 |
| **Finish** | Kowloon Reservoir bus stop, Tai Po Road 九龍水塘巴士站, 大埔公路 |
| **Distance** | 16km |
| **Total ascent** | 1270m |
| **Grade** | Difficult |
| **Time** | 6hr |
| **Terrain** | Begins with stone steps along an ancient path, followed by dirt paths and quiet roads, and finishes with a long segment by a catchwater |
| **Summits** | Tung Shan (544m) |

Section 4 is glorious, despite an inauspicious beginning. Once through the village and allotment area, the ancient stone path makes a great ascent through the wild, quiet beauty of dense green woodlands. The scenery changes dramatically towards the summit of Tung Shan, with great viewpoints. This is followed by lovely easy walking in Section 5, mostly by a catchwater, where it is possible to see deer, monkeys and many birds. As it is rather flat, the exhilarating optional extra to Amah Rock adds challenge and mythical interest.

**Public transport for Day 3**

**Beginning:** From Choi Hung MTR station (Kwun Tong line) exit C2, take bus 91, 92, 91M, or 91P.

**To finish or start at Section 4/5 junction:** With no public transport, it is easier to join Sections 4 and 5. Alternatively, pre-book a taxi if you want to finish here. To start here, take a taxi to Lion's Pavilion, Sha Tin Pass Road 獅子亭, 沙田坳道.

**End:** Take bus 81 to Prince Edward or Mong Kok MTR stations (Tsuen Wan and Kwun Tong lines).

There is a store 100 metres from the bus stop along Clear Water Bay Road.

## Section 4

From the bus stop, follow the road heading E and take the first left-hand turn after 30 metres, signed Tseng Lan Shue village. ◄ Veer left immediately after a pagoda, taking the NW footpath on the left of the village playground. Turn right after the basketball court, cross the storm drain and immediately turn left. At a T-junction 150 metres later, turn right then immediately left, cross another storm drain and turn right. After 150 metres on the concrete path, turn right onto a dirt track. There are minimal Wilson Trail signs in the village, but there is a

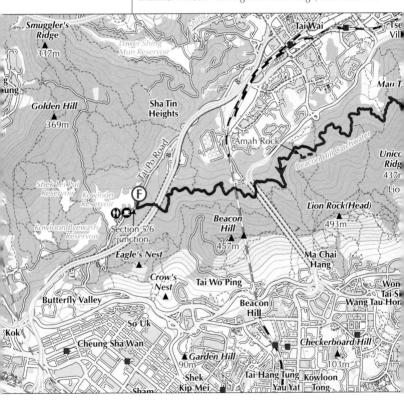

signboard here for Stage 4 (although the official start is back at Clear Water Bay Road).

There follows one of the unexpected delights of the trail, walking up an ancient stone path into a densely wooded area, very quiet, clean and beautiful, like a true rainforest. Cross over a couple of streams and pass a disused garden nursery; after 1.3km of forest walking, reach a junction and go right, signed Ho Chung. Ignore any turnings and continue on the path for 200 metres to **Tai Lam Wu Road** 大藍湖路. Turn left, still signed Ho Chung, and continue for 600 metres, ignoring any turnings. Cross

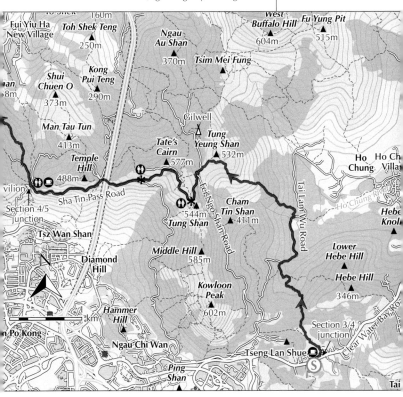

*Ancient footpath*

a catchwater by a bridge on the left, take steps up and subsequently follow signs for Ngau Liu.

Fork left 100 metres later, from concrete onto dirt track. After a good ascent of 1.5km, the trail follows the contours around **Tung Yeung Shan** 東洋山 and reaches a tarmac road 400 metres later. ◄ Follow the road left and uphill for 100 metres to a T-junction. Go right, uphill, onto **Fei Ngo Shan Road** (飛鵝山道 literally means Flying Goose Hill Road, although the English name of this hill is Kowloon Peak).

Follow the road for 500 metres to **Tung Shan** (東山 East Hill). ◄ Continue walking along the road for about 1km to a road junction and go straight ahead onto **Sha**

Gilwell campsite is nearby but only available for large groups.

There are two Kowloon Peak viewpoints here.

134

**Tin Pass Road** 沙田坳道. Follow this for 1.7km to **Lion's Pavilion** 獅子亭, a pagoda with two concrete lions. This is the **Section 4/5 junction**. ▶

There is a store here.

## Section 5

From the pavilion, turn right (N), signed Shap Yi Wat Village. The road immediately forks; go left, and shortly afterwards there is a Wilson Trail signboard. Then fork right after 250 metres (left is to Shap Yi Wat Village), and shortly thereafter cross a bridge and immediately turn right onto a concrete track. Follow the main path for 1.3km to the start of **Beacon Hill Catchwater**. Follow this for a long way, thinking, 'How delightful to walk along the level with no steps!' At 2.3km along, there is a left-hand turn signed **Amah Rock**, an optional extra.

### Optional extra to the legendary Amah Rock

This adds 0.8km, 50m ascent and 20min. Take the left-hand signed turn, cross the catchwater then shortly afterwards fork right. It is well signposted all the way to the top, where you are rewarded by superb views over all of the New Territories. Retrace your steps to the trail.

> *Amah* means 'mother' in many different Asian languages, but the Chinese name is 望夫石, meaning **Looking out for Husband Rock**. The legend is that a woman waited for a long, long time at this high viewpoint for her fisherman husband to return from afar. The Goddess Mazu took pity on her, because the woman's husband had drowned at sea, and turned her and the baby on her back into this 15m-tall rock.

### Main route

Walk along the easy-to-follow catchwater for a total of 6.3km (with no landmarks) to its end. Go straight ahead towards **Tai Po Road**, which is the **Section 5/6 junction**. Turn right onto a raised concrete path just before reaching the road, leading to a footbridge. To complete today's itinerary, do not cross the bridge but go down the steps to Kowloon Reservoir bus stop. ▶

To continue the trail, cross the bridge, head NE along Tai Po Road and take the first left turn onto a footpath at a Wilson Trail signboard.

# DAY 4
## *Kowloon Reservoir to Tai Wo*

| | |
|---|---|
| **Start** | Kowloon Reservoir bus stop, Tai Po Road 九龍水塘巴士站, 大埔公路 |
| **Finish** | Tai Wo MTR station (East Rail line) 太和港鐵站 |
| **Distance** | 20.5km |
| **Total ascent** | 1080m |
| **Grade** | Difficult |
| **Time** | 6hr 45min |
| **Terrain** | A mixture of dirt paths and quiet maintenance roads, with a long easy dirt path around the reservoir, finishing with an urban section |

Section 6 is a relatively short hike from Kowloon Reservoir to Shing Mun Reservoir via forested paths. Section 7 is a lovely easy walk around Shing Mun Reservoir along beautiful verdant shaded paths with views of water and much birdsong. Both sections are suitable for families, especially to see monkeys or look out for wild boar. Section 8 goes through suburban villages via old ways, with views down onto the bustling urban areas.

Halfway through Section 8, the trail goes very close to an MTR station. This is a convenient point at which to end the day's itinerary, as splitting the section solves the problem of it ending without access to transport.

**Public transport for Day 4**

**Beginning:** From Prince Edward MTR station (Tsuen Wan and Kwun Tong lines) exit E, head N along Nathan Road for 50 metres and take bus 81.

**To finish at Section 6/7 junction:** Turn left (W) before the main dam, go down the road signed 'maxicab' and follow it for 1.5km to Shing Mun Country Park Visitor Centre (with a kiosk). Take green minibus 82 to the terminus on Shiu Wo Street, then go NE down an alleyway (signed MTR). Turn right at its end, go up an escalator and cross two roads via a pedestrian walkway leading to Tsuen Wan MTR station (Tsuen Wan line) 荃灣港鐵站.

**To start at Section 6/7 junction:** From Tsuen Wan MTR station (Tsuen Wan line) exit B1, cross two roads via a pedestrian bridge, turn right, descend to Castle Peak Road, then take the first left down an alleyway to Shiu Wo Street; the minibus terminus is to the left. Take green minibus 82 to the terminus at Shing Mun Reservoir 城門水塘. From the minibus stop, walk SW up the road (away from Shing Mun Country Park Visitor Centre) to reach the main dam after 1.5km.

**To finish at Section 7/8 junction:** From San Uk Ka minibus stop, take green minibus 23S or 23K to Tai Po Market MTR station (East Rail line) 大埔墟港 鐵站.

**To start at Section 7/8 junction:** Take green minibus 23S or 23K from Tai Po Market MTR station (East Rail line) to San Uk Ka minibus stop (terminus).

## Section 6

From the bus stop, walk back along the road (SW) then almost immediately take the first right-hand footpath with a Wilson Trail signboard. Walk along the reservoir's edge and the path becomes a maintenance road. After a short distance, turn left, then 250 metres later go up the steps.

Rapidly leaving the traffic noise behind, walk along a lovely path through dense subtropical woodland for 1.3km. Take the first footpath on the right, and about 1km later turn right onto **Golden Hill Road** 金山路. ▶ Take the second turning on the right after 200 metres, and go up the steps. Follow this main path for 2km, ignoring a right-hand turn towards the end, and arrive at **Shing Mun Reservoir** 城門水塘. The official **Section 6/7 junction** is across the main **dam**.

This quiet maintenance road is also part of MacLehose Trail.

The names around **Shing Mun** have an interesting history. Shing Mun, meaning Fort Gate, is so named as it was the site of a Ming Dynasty military base. The reservoir (built 1933–37) was originally named Jubilee Reservoir after King George V's Silver Jubilee (1935). The dam by the Visitor Centre is called Pineapple Dam because there were once many pineapple orchards around here.

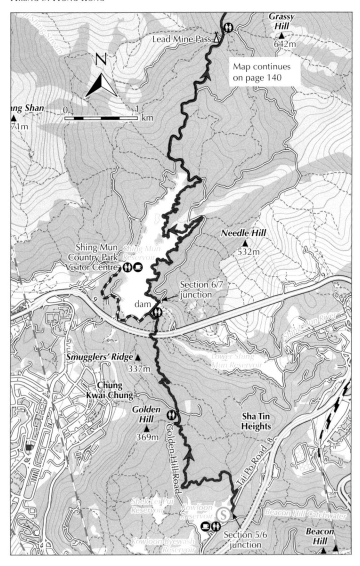

*Grassy Hill* ▲ 642m

Lead Mine Pass △

Map continues on page 140

N

0 — 1 km

*ng Shan* ▲ 71m

*Needle Hill* ▲ 532m

Shing Mun Country Park Visitor Centre

*Shing Mun Reservoir*

Section 6/7 junction

dam

*Smugglers' Ridge* ▲ 337m

*Upper Shing Mun Reservoir*

Chung Kwai Chung

*Golden Hill* ▲ 369m

*Sha Tin Heights*

Golden Hill Road

Tai Po Road 8

Shing Mun River

*Shek Lei Pui Reservoir*

*Kowloon Reservoir*

S

Section 5/6 junction

*Beacon Hill Catchwater*

*Kowloon Byewash Reservoir*

*Beacon Hill* ▲

138

*The resident monkeys*

However, the area is now locally known as **Monkey Hill** because of the resident monkey population. Macaques were introduced here to control the poisonous strychnine plants spreading around the reservoirs in the early 1900s. Today, people come to feed the monkeys, although it is illegal; the thousands of animals are viewed either as a nuisance (because they steal food and are not toilet-trained) or as cute.

## Section 7

Walk across the main **dam** (which is also MacLehose Trail), and turn left to walk along the shore of **Shing Mun Reservoir**, a lovely, quiet, shaded, green track. After 5km, reach a concrete road and turn left.

The trees here are spectacularly large and ancient because they are the remnants of the *feng shui* grove of **Shing Mun Lo Wai** (Shing Mun Old Village). The villagers were relocated in 1926 before the area was flooded during the reservoir's construction.

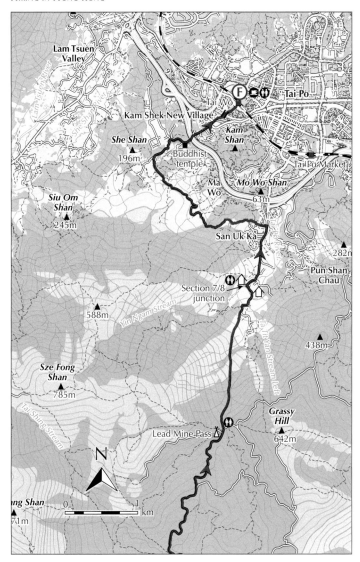

*Feng shui* woodlands can be seen at several sites around Hong Kong; they are all that remain of long-abandoned villages, where trees were nurtured by local people to bring good luck and keep evil spirits at bay.

At a T-junction 600 metres later, go right, signed Tai Po and Lead Mine Pass. Follow this road for 1.4km to a fork and go left, uphill. About 1km later is **Lead Mine Pass campsite** 鉛礦坳營地. Go right at the fork, signed Tai Po, then a very short distance later, arrive at Lead Mine Pass. Leave the road and take a small footpath to the left of the **toilets**. Follow this path down for 1.6km to a road and turn left. At the second **shelter** 400 metres later is the official **Section 7/8 junction**. Continue on the road, past some toilets to a T-junction, turn right downhill, and 500 metres later is **San Uk Ka** minibus stop 新屋家小巴站.

### Section 8 (first part)
Walk down the main road (Wun Yiu Road) for 600 metres and take the road on the left signed Wun Yiu kiln site. ▶ At the top of the road 100 metres later, when it

*The beginning of Section 7 at Shing Mun Reservoir*

There is a very small Wilson Trail sign here, which is easy to miss.

*The local fishermen moor their boats under the covered bridge in Tai Wo*

turns 90 degrees right, take the footpath straight ahead signed Ma Wo. Less than 100 metres later, fork right uphill (well signed), and stay on the main path, now on old ways going up and up for 800 metres. Reach a road and follow it, signed Cloudy Hill.

After 1.5km, arrive at a T-junction and turn right, downhill, along Shek Lin Road. About 500 metres later, go past a large **Buddhist temple** on the right, then the route goes underneath a major highway. At a taxi stand 350 metres later, turn left, signed Cloudy Hill. Almost immediately, as the road curves left, go straight ahead into the pedestrianised **Kam Shek New Village** 錦石新村 (signs are intermittent).

Veer right, staying to the left of the playground, and 200 metres along walk over the traditional Chinese covered **bridge** crossing the Lam Tsuen River. ◄ To finish today's itinerary, go straight ahead following MTR signs, up the steps and into the shopping mall for **Tai Wo MTR station**.

*To continue the trail, go left (NW) at the end of the bridge, following the banks of the river, signed Cloudy Hill.*

# DAY 5
*Tai Wo to Nam Chung*

| | |
|---|---|
| **Start** | Tai Wo MTR station (East Rail line) 太和港鐵站 |
| **Finish** | Nam Chung Lee Uk village bus stop, Luk Keng Road 南涌李屋村巴士站, 鹿頸路 |
| **Distance** | 23km (short version: 12.25km) |
| **Total ascent** | 1470m (short version: 910m) |
| **Grade** | Challenging (short version: difficult) |
| **Time** | 9hr (short version: 5hr) |
| **Terrain** | Urban for a short while, followed by many steps to Cloudy Hill, then excellent dirt paths leading to a massive ridge walk; after a steep descent, the route is mostly on ancient paths |
| **Summits** | Yuk Sau Fung (290m), Cloudy Hill (440m), the eight summits of Pat Sin Leng: Shun Yeung Fung (590m), Chung Li Fung (529m), Kao Lao Fung (543m), Kuai Li Fung (522m), Tsao Kau Fung (508m), Choi Wo Fung (489m), Sheung Tsz Fung (513m), Hsien Ku Fung (511m); optional: Wong Leng (639m), Lai Pek Shan (550m) |

A long, challenging and exhilarating day of summits! After a short urban portion, there is a significant, endurance-testing ascent via many steps to finish the second part of Section 8 at the lovely summit of Cloudy Hill, entering Pat Sin Leng Country Park. Section 9 encompasses beautiful woodland around a reservoir, leading to open grassland around Ping Fung Shan. This is followed by two optional summits and then the eight peaks of Pat Sin Leng mountain range – truly the finest ridge walk of Hong Kong.

The tenth and final section begins with a long steep descent before following some delightful ancient paths in shaded greenery, with streams, rocky pools and ruined villages. The day concludes at Nam Chung village, walking among mangrove-lined fish ponds.

Both Sections 8 and 9 end with neither public transport nor road access, hence are best linked together with Section 10. Alternatively, the short version encompasses most of Section 9, the best part of today's itinerary.

## Public transport for Day 5

**To finish or start at Section 8/9 junction:** With neither road access nor public transport, Section 8 is best linked with Sections 9 and 10. Alternatively, follow Wilson Trail to or from Tai Wo MTR station (4.5km).

**Day 5 short version start:** From Fanling MTR (East Rail line) exit C, take green minibus 52B to the terminus at Hok Tau.

**Day 5 short version finish:** Take bus 75K or green minibus 20C to Tai Po Market MTR station (East Rail line).

**To finish or start at Section 9/10 junction:** The only way to and from here is on foot.

**End:** Take green minibus 56K to Fanling MTR station (East Rail line) 粉嶺港鐵站.

### Section 8 (second part)

From Tai Wo MTR station exit A, inside the shopping mall, go left, down the escalator or steps, then go straight ahead to the river (do not cross the traditional **covered bridge**). Turn right and head NW along the river. At the next **pedestrian bridge** 400 metres later, turn right, away from the bridge, following signs for Cloudy Hill.

Reach a road and turn left, then 250 metres later at its end, cross over the main road at the traffic lights. Turn right then immediate left to go through an underpass beneath the railway (no sign). Thereafter, turn right, then 20 metres later turn left onto Tai Po Tau Drive, signed Cloudy Hill. Follow the road for 400 metres, and after it has curved left, take the footpath on the right to go up the steps.

An ascent of 500 metres leads to an unnamed trig point, and 900 metres later, at the fourth shelter on this ascent, leave the main path onto a dirt track on the right (E), signed Cloudy Hill. After 500 metres, arrive at the summit of **Yuk Sau Fung** (玉秀峰 Exquisite-as-Jade Peak). This is followed by a daunting set of stairs to climb and an excellent ridge walk of 1.2km, leading to another path.

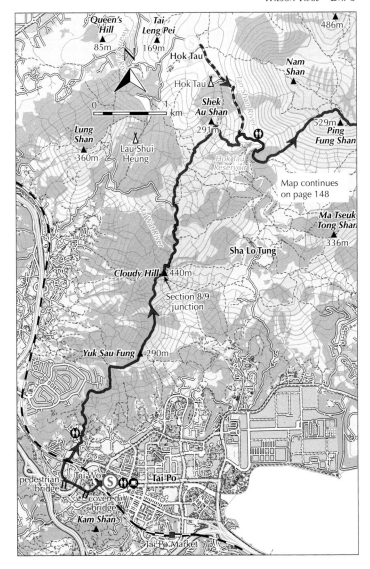

Queen's Hill
85m

Tai Leng Pei
169m

Hok Tau

Hok Tau △

Nam Shan ▲

Shek Au Shan
291m

Tai Shan River

529m ▲
Ping Fung Shan

Lung Shan ▲
360m

Lau Shui Heung △

Hok Tau Reservoir

Map continues on page 148

Ma Wat River

Ma Tseuk Tong Shan ▲
336m

Sha Lo Tung

Cloudy Hill ▲ 440m

Section 8/9 junction

Yuk Sau Fung ▲ 290m

pedestrian bridge

Tai Wo

S

Tai Po

covered bridge

Kam Shan ▲

Tai Po Market

145

*There are a lot of steps to Cloudy Hill*

The Chinese name of Cloudy Hill is 九龍坑山, Kau Lung Hang Shan, meaning Kowloon Trench Hill.

Lau Shui Heung campsite is 2km off the trail from here.

The Day 5 short version joins here, and Hok Tau campsite is 1km off the trail.

Turn right, and 100 metres later arrive at the aerial-festooned summit of **Cloudy Hill**, which is the **Section 8/9 junction**. ◀

## Section 9
With **Cloudy Hill** summit on the right, continue NE on the main path, through a lovely shaded green tunnel in what is now Pat Sin Leng Country Park. At a footpath crossroads 1.1km later, go straight ahead, signed Lau Shui Heung Reservoir (the trail does not go there). ◀ After about 1km, turn right downhill, signed Hok Tau Reservoir. (Ignore confusing signs: one Wilson Trail sign says straight ahead, immediately followed by another one saying go right.) Walk along for 1km, admiring the impressive preview of the ridge to come. At the bottom of some steps near Hok Tau Reservoir, turn left, signed Hok Tau, and 150 metres later reach **Hok Tau Reservoir 鶴藪水塘**. ◀

### Day 5 short version: from Hok Tau to the main trail
From the bus terminus at Hok Tau, head SE along the quiet maintenance road for 1.5km (the barrier is for cars,

not people), ascending along a lovely valley to **Hok Tau Reservoir**, where you join the main trail. ▸

Cross the dam, then curve right to walk along the road by the reservoir's edge. At the end of the road 500 metres later, take the footpath on the left, signed Pat Sin Range. Walk for 50 metres to the end of the barbecue area then turn left up the steps (same sign); in about 300 metres, turn left up more steps (same sign).

Ascend for 1km, then suddenly the woodland becomes shrubland and the path becomes less steep. Continue walking around the summit of **Ping Fung Shan** (屏風山 Screen Hill), noticing the very unusual path of bare white rock.

> The soft white rock gives a fascinating insight into Hong Kong's geological past. It is **calcareous silt-stone**, laid down in the Carboniferous era 300 million years ago, which is only formed in shallow freshwater lakes, close to the shore.

After about 450 metres, arrive at a crossroads very near to the crest of a ridge and go straight ahead, signed

From here, the main trail and the Day 5 short version follow the same route to the steps after Hsien Ku Fung summit.

*White rock path on the finest ridge walk of Hong Kong*

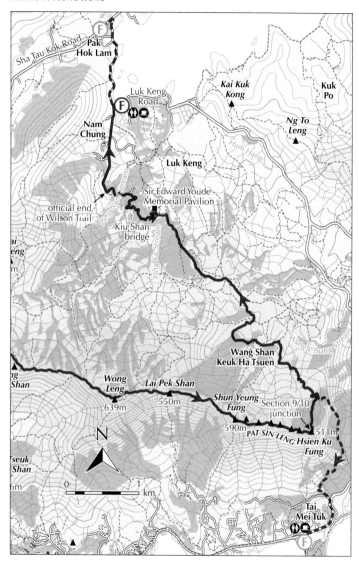

Pat Sin Leng, to walk along the ridge. ▶ Arrive 1.7km later at a turning on the right for the summit of **Wong Leng**.

This long ridge is simply stunning, showcasing Hong Kong's greenery and rural tranquillity.

### Optional extra: Wong Leng

Wong Leng 黃嶺 (Yellow Peak) is the 15th highest hill in Hong Kong. The trig point is only 50 metres from the turning. After visiting, retrace your steps.

Continue along the ridge walk, enjoying amazing views: ahead, the path snakes fantastically onwards towards Double Haven Bay with its striking red rocks, to the right is Plover Cove (Walk 8) and the 76m-tall statue of the Bodhisattva, while to the left is mainland China across the waters. After about 800 metres, arrive at a minor crest with a turning on the right for another optional summit.

*Looking back at Wong Leng and Lai Pek Shan*

## Optional extra: Lai Pek Shan

The summit of **Lai Pek Shan** is only 20 metres away. The path could be slightly overgrown because it is infrequently visited; it is a good spot for a break. Retrace your steps to the trail.

Continue along for just over 1km, then the ridge walk gets even better when the trail arrives at **Shun Yeung Fung**, the first summit of Pat Sin Leng and the 19th highest in Hong Kong. This is followed by **Chung Li Fung**, **Kao Lao Fung**, **Kuai Li Fung**, **Tsao Kau Fung**, **Choi Wo Fung** and **Sheung Tsz Fung**, then, 1.2km after it began, Pat Sin Leng finishes at the trig point of **Hsien Ku Fung**. ◄ This is the **Section 9/10 junction**.

*Hsien Ku Fung is the 45th highest summit in Hong Kong and the only one named after a female immortal.*

## PAT SIN LENG RANGE

The mountain range of Pat Sin Leng (八仙嶺 Eight Immortals Ridge) has eight summits, each named after one of the legendary eight immortals of Chinese mythology: a woman, a disabled person, a rich general, a young scholar, an old man, a beggar, a high government official, and a prince – eight people born about 4000 years ago representing all walks of life, who were magically transcended into immortals. Throughout Chinese history, they have appeared in murals and stories, representing prosperity and longevity. The most well-known stories include 'Eight Immortals Crossing the Sea' and 'Eight Immortals Wishing the Heavenly Queen Happy Birthday'.

## Section 10

There is only one route down, heading N, signed Bride's Pool and Tai Mei Tuk. Go down the steps to reach a junction 500 metres later. ◄

*The Day 5 short version leaves the main trail here.*

### Day 5 short version: from the main trail to Tai Mei Tuk

At the junction, turn right (SE), signed Tai Mei Tuk. Follow the main path for 2km, then cross over a catchwater to a quiet maintenance road. Turn left, downhill, and reach Ting Kok Road after 100 metres. Go right, downhill (S), for 600 metres and **Tai Mei Tuk** bus terminus 大美督巴士總站 is on the right.

**Main route**

To continue the main trail, turn left at the junction, signed Bride's Pool. Continue along this welcome, easy-walking section for 1.2km, crossing some pretty streams shaded by bamboo and shrubbery, and then take an easy-to-miss footpath on the left, signed Nam Chung (no longer following signs for Bride's Pool). ▶

Just 250 metres further on, arrive at the ruins of the abandoned lower village of **Wang Shan Keuk Ha Tsuen**, followed 500 metres later by the even more beautiful ruins of the upper village; here, you are walking on the ancient way through *feng shui* woods (see Section 7), full of giant, ancient trees.

At a footpath crossroads 500 metres later, go straight ahead. Ignore any turnings for 2km, reach a cemetery, turn left signed Nam Chung and Sir Edward Youde Memorial Pavilion. Just 50 metres later, still within the cemetery, take an easily missed left fork. Note a turning

*Approaching one of the eight summits of Pat Sin Leng*

This is Wang Shan Ancient Path.

151

on the right 50 metres later for the optional viewpoint at **Sir Edward Youde Memorial Pavilion**.

> The beautiful **pavilion** commemorates Sir Edward Youde, Governor of Hong Kong 1982–86, who died in office. The views from the pavilion are sublime. (The pavilion is 100 metres from the turning; after visiting, retrace your steps to the trail.)

Continue on the main route for 200 metres, cross over **Kiu Shan Bridge** (admire the ruins of the old bridge on the left), then reach a road after 130 metres. Follow the road for just over 1km to the **official end of Wilson Trail**, at the border of the country park. Keep following the road and arrive 500 metres later at **Nam Chung** village. ◄ Stroll along for 800 metres next to peaceful fish ponds and mangroves, and reach a T-junction which is the end of the walk. The minibus stop is to the right, in front of the shelter on **Luk Keng Road**. ◄

**Alternative finish**
Turn left at Luk Keng Road and walk another 1.3km to **Sha Tau Kok Road**. The bus stop is on the left after 100 metres. Take bus 78K or 277A to Fanling MTR station.

This remote village used to have a population of more than 200, but now there are only 15 aged residents.

The minibus is infrequent and often full: see alternative below. There is a café/store and toilets nearby.

# DAY WALKS

The 'old way' after Hang Mei Teng (Walk 14)

# WALK 1
## *Big Knife Mountain*

| | |
|---|---|
| **Start** | Kadoorie Farm bus stop, Lam Kam Road 嘉道理農場巴士站, 林錦路 |
| **Finish** | Fanling MTR station (East Rail line) 粉嶺港鐵站 |
| **Distance** | 8.75km |
| **Total ascent** | 560m |
| **Grade** | Moderate |
| **Time** | 3hr 30min |
| **Terrain** | A mixture of stone and concrete steps, dirt, stone and concrete paths, plus pavement |
| **Summits** | Tai To Yan (Big Knife Mountain, 566m), Pak Tai To Yan (480m), Kei Lak Tsai (256m) |
| **Map** | North West New Territories |

Tai To Yan 大刀屻, meaning Big Knife Blade, is a mountain named after its shape. This is a lovely ridge walk that is relatively short and easy, with great views of Shenzhen in China, Pat Sin Leng mountain range (Wilson Trail, Section 9), Plover Cove Reservoir (Walk 8), and Hong Kong's highest mountain, Tai Mo Shan (MacLehose Trail, Section 8).

The walk starts opposite Kadoorie Farm, which is a working farm, botanic garden and educational centre that every Hong Kong schoolchild will have visited. It ends at one of Hong Kong's most famous temples, Fung Ying Seen Koon. These two additional attractions make the route a 'grand day out' for the whole family.

## Public transport

**Beginning:** From Kam Sheung Road MTR station (Tuen Ma line) exit C, take bus 64K (direction Tai Po Market).

From the bus stop, head N along the path, plunging into Lam Tsuen Country Park. Follow the main path through

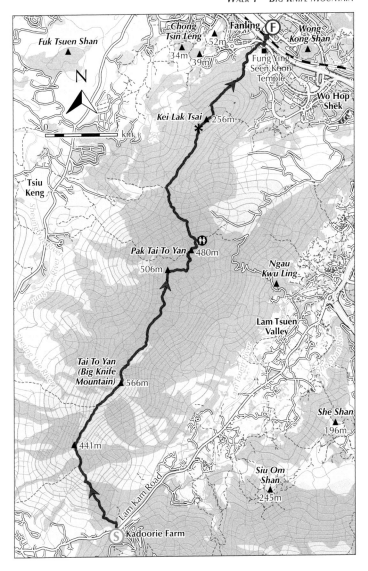

*Looking back in the silvery morning light at Tai Mo Shan*

Take a breath and look behind to see Tai Mo Shan and the many peaks of MacLehose and Wilson Trails, hopefully backlit by the silvery early morning light.

jungle-like foliage for 100 metres then take the first left-hand path up the steps, signed Fanling station via Tai To Yan. Enjoy the climb for 1km, steep but not arduous, leading to an **unnamed peak** (441m, no trig point). ◄

Now walk along one of Hong Kong's phenomenal ridge walks for 1.4km to the summit of **Tai To Yan** (Big Knife Mountain). Follow the main path, now in dense subtropical woodland underplanted with ferns, arriving 1.8km later at another **unnamed peak** (506m, no trig point). Continue on the obvious main path for 600 metres to the trig point of **Pak Tai To Yan** (北大刀岃 North Big Knife Blade).

About 200 metres later, go left at a fork, then arrive at a **toilet** and fork left again, signed Fanling station. At a footpath T-junction after 150 metres, go left (same sign), then nearly 1km later fork right near some concrete benches (same sign). This immediately forks: take either option as they shortly rejoin, then pass several shelters and a **viewpoint**, arriving 1km later at **Kei Lak Tsai** 箕勒仔 (trig point but no view).

To encourage people to use the country parks for fresh air and exercise, the Agriculture, Fisheries and Conservation Department maintains **trails and outdoor facilities**, including many shelters as seen on this walk, essential in the heat of high summer. Hongkongers now (in 2022) have a life expectancy of 85 years, compared to 81 in the UK, which goes to show that exercise is good!

Just 150 metres along, after the sixth shelter on this ridge, turn left down the steps signed Fanling station and Wu Tip Shan Path. Pass many more shelters, usually filled with Hongkongers exercising, and reach a crossroads 600 metres later. Go straight ahead, and at the bottom of the trail shortly afterwards continue onwards following signs for Wah Ming Tsuen. Fork right after 600 metres signed Fanling station, leading to a main road. To the right is **Fung Ying Seen Koon Temple 蓬瀛仙館**. Cross to the other side of the road, leading directly to **Fanling MTR station**.

**Fung Ying Seen Koon Temple** is the most important Tao temple complex in Hong Kong. The Chinese name refers to the legendary wonderland where the immortals live, and the temple attempts to recreate this paradise on earth. Built in 1929 utilising traditional building techniques, it consists of three eye-catching individual temples, although most worshippers are interested in the Inscribed Wall of Tao Te Ching or the impressive 12 bronze statues of the Chinese horoscope.

# WALK 2
*Tai Lam Chung Reservoir Circuit*

| | |
|---|---|
| **Start/Finish** | Tsing Lung Tau minibus terminus, Lung Yue Road 青龍頭 小巴站, 龍如路 |
| **Distance** | 22.5km |
| **Total ascent** | 1200m |
| **Grade** | Difficult |
| **Time** | 6hr 30min |
| **Terrain** | Gentle undulating mixture of stone and concrete steps, road and pavement, plus dirt, stone and concrete paths |
| **Map** | North West New Territories |

This route combines Tai Lam and Yuen Tun Country Trails into a circular walk, enjoying the countryside of the Tai Lam Chung valley, which was flooded to create Tai Lam Chung Reservoir. This was the first reservoir to be built after World War 2, the largest at that time in Hong Kong, drowning several villages which used to be linked by Yuen Tsuen Ancient Trail (Walk 3). The reservoir is also known as Thousand Islands Lake because of its myriad irregularly scalloped islands. On some of the islands, the ruined remnants of villages are revealed when the water level is low.

This is a relatively easy low-level walk (all inclines are gentle – it is graded as difficult mainly because of the long distance), mostly in shade through subtropical greenery. It includes a long stretch around the reservoir and is suitable for anyone who would like a very long walk without undue pressure on the knees. The optional extra provides historical interest.

## Public transport

**Beginning:** From Tsuen Wan MTR station (Tsuen Wan line) exit B, turn left and cross the second bridge on the right (labelled as B2 exit although it is not within the station). Then take the first left followed by the first right and go down steps on the right, signed with pictures of minibus and taxi. Take minibus 96M.

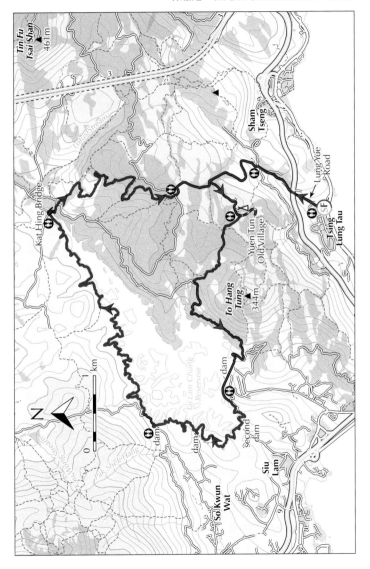

From the minibus terminus, walk up **Lung Yue Road** for 1km, going beneath a main highway, past Tai Lam Country Park sign and **toilets**, then turn left up a quiet road signed Yuen Tun Country Trail. Follow this road up for 1km, then take a left-hand road signed Yuen Tun Country Trail and CAS Yuen Tun Camp.

> CAS stands for **Civil Aid Services**, whose routine duties include patrolling the country parks and managing crowds at major events. They also provide mountain search and rescue (which hopefully you will not require!) plus disaster relief.

About 700 metres later, fork right, arriving 150 metres later at **Yuen Tun Camp** main gate (toilets on left, camping not available to the general public). To continue the trail, turn right (NW), signed Yuen Tun Country Trail. Alternatively, an optional diversion to Yuen Tun Old Village begins here.

### Optional extra to Yuen Tun Old Village

This adds 0.7km, negligible ascent and 15min. Go through the **Yuen Tun Camp** main gate, and 150 metres later pass an oriental garden with a man-made lotus pond. Follow the road for a further 200 metres to **Yuen Tun Old Village** (圓墩 Round Mound). This is an abandoned Hakka village, whose residents were relocated when their land was flooded. Some houses have been preserved, with exhibits inside including furniture and agricultural tools, giving people an idea of the lifestyle of the Hakka. (See Walk 6 for more about the Hakka people.) After visiting, retrace your steps to the **Yuen Tun Camp** main gate.

Head NW from the main gate, then after 500 metres go straight ahead at a footpath crossroads, following signs for Yuen Tun Country Trail and Tai Lam Chung Reservoir. Continue along this lovely shaded path through a densely forested area, cross a river, then after 750 metres fork left, signed Castle Peak Road (leaving Yuen

Tun Country Trail). Reach a quiet maintenance road 300 metres later, and go left, signed Tai Lam and Castle Peak Road.

After 400 metres, arrive at a T-junction and go left (NW), still signed Castle Peak Road. Walk along the road parallel to the shoreline of **Tai Lam Chung Reservoir** for just over 1km. Reach a T-junction with another road, go right, follow the road to a **dam** and cross it. At the end of the dam, fork right, through a picnic area with **toilets**, now following signs for Siu Lam, Castle Peak Road (mountain bike trail). About 800 metres further, at the end of the **second dam**, continue on the main path following signs for Pak Shek Hang (not to Siu Lam down steps on the left).

After 600 metres, fork right, signed Wong Nai Tun Reservoir. Continue along the sandy trails through low scrubby pines for 600 metres, then at a footpath T-junction go right. Shortly thereafter, cross another **dam**, and fork right (same sign). Continue along for 1km, cross one more **dam** and reach a quiet maintenance road. Turn right, uphill. ▶

*Oriental garden on the way to Yuen Tun Old Village*

This is also MacLehose Trail.

*Thousand Islands Lake nestled in the lush green Tai Lam Chung valley*

Stay on the road for 300 metres then go down steps on the right, signed Tai Lam Chung Reservoir Mountain Bike Trail (a shared use path). Follow the trail for 3km as it goes around the reservoir, past a particularly beautiful river with pools and through a shaded valley. Twice the path forks but both options soon rejoin. Next, ignore a left turn for Wong Nai Tun Reservoir and stay on the main path for 2km, now following signs for Tin Fu Tsai, through an area of astounding bamboo clumps.

Arrive at a bridge and cross over to reach the top of the reservoir. Turn right immediately and go through a picnic area, then cross **Kat Hing Bridge** 吉慶橋. Turn right (no sign) and follow an unofficial, narrow, rough footpath as it curves right then slopes up to a road 200 metres along. Cross directly over the road and head up the path on the other side, signed Yuen Tun Country Trail and Tsing Fai Tong.

After 400 metres, merge with Yuen Tsuen Ancient Trail (Walk 3) then fork right after 50 metres, away from it, now following Yuen Tun Country Trail signs. At a footpath T-junction 1km later, go right (same sign). In just over 1km, go straight ahead at a footpath crossroads (same sign). At a multiway junction 1km later, leave the Yuen Tun Country Trail and go first left up steps (SE) signed Tsing Lung Tau, arriving 100 metres later at a road with a traffic island and three-way junction.

Go straight across the island then down the road (SE), still following signs for Tsing Lung Tau. Follow this for nearly 2km (rejoining the outward route after 750 metres) back to Tai Lam Country Park entrance, turn right and retrace your steps to **Tsing Lung Tau** minibus terminus.

*Tawny rajah (butterfly)*

163

# WALK 3
*Yuen Tsuen Ancient Trail*

| | |
|---|---|
| **Start** | Tsuen Wan Adventist Hospital bus stop 港安醫院巴士站 |
| **Finish** | Tai Tong Shan Road bus stop, Kiu Hing Road 大棠山道巴士站, 僑興路 |
| **Distance** | 14.5km |
| **Total ascent** | 730m |
| **Grade** | Moderate |
| **Time** | 4hr 30min |
| **Terrain** | A mixture of stone and concrete steps, pavement, and dirt, stone and concrete paths |
| **Summits** | Shek Lung Kung (474m); optional: Ha Fa Shan (315m) |
| **Map** | North West New Territories |

Yuen Tsuen Ancient Trail is a 400-year-old route linking two settlements, Yuen Long and Tsuen Wan. There are many more old routes in the area, and villagers used to depend on them to get to the market town of Tsuen Wan to sell their agricultural produce. Many villages were relocated when Tai Lam Chung Reservoir was built in the 1950s, flooding part of the valley. Nature has since taken over, making this route amazingly green and lush, almost jungle-like.

The path is relatively easy walking, with two summits, views of a famous modern bridge and a serene-looking reservoir; however, it would have been hard work for villagers carrying their heavy market goods.

## Public transport

**Beginning:** From Tsuen Wan MTR station (Tsuen Wan line) exit A1, take the pedestrian bridge over two roads, descend along the spiral walkway to the road, turn left and left again to get to Castle Peak Road, then arrive at Fu Wah bus stop. Take bus 39M, 30 or 30X.

**End:** Take bus K66 to Yuet Ping House, Long Ping Estate bus stop. Long Ping MTR station (Tuen Ma line) is directly ahead up the steps.

Many **ramshackle buildings** are to be seen on the first part of this trail. Squatters have existed in Hong Kong since 1844, and by the 1950s it was estimated that up to 25 per cent of the population were living in structures built without planning permission. In 1982, the government found 100,000 such dwellings during a territory-wide survey. Those registered at that time remained officially illegal but were allowed to stand on a temporary basis, with no right of sale or rebuilding. The residents were encouraged to apply for public housing, resulting in a gradual decline in numbers.

*Juxtaposition of greenery and concrete landscape*

Go up the road (W) for 50 metres and take the steps on the left, signed Yuen Tsuen Ancient Trail. After 400 metres, arrive at a catchwater, cross it to a shelter and go up the path (same sign). Turn right after 250 metres (same

165

sign), then 500 metres later, after passing some agricultural terracing, reach a concrete path crossroads by a **shelter**; turn left (SW) to continue the trail. An optional detour to Ha Fa Shan summit begins here.

**Optional summit: Ha Fa Shan**
This adds 0.75km, 50m ascent and 20min. Take an unsigned rough path on the right behind the shelter. It

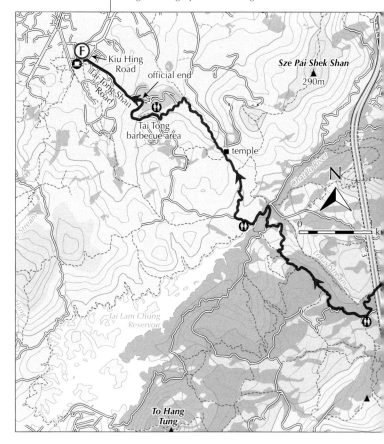

immediately forks; both forks go to the same place, but right is quicker. Fork right again after 200 metres, then 200 metres further arrive at the summit of **Ha Fa Shan** (下花山 Downwards Flower Hill). After enjoying the superb views of Hong Kong's highest mountain, Tai Mo Shan (MacLehose Trail, Section 8), retrace your steps to the main trail.

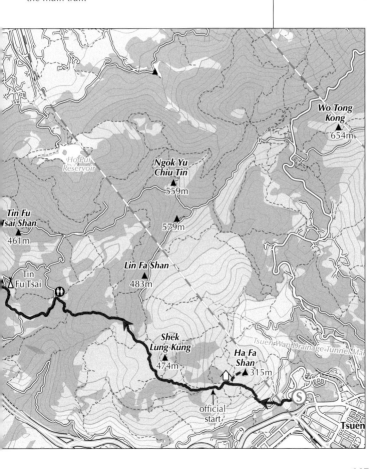

*The summit of Ha Fa Shan with Tai Mo Shan in the background*

**Main route**

Head SW from the path crossroads, and 150 metres later arrive at the **official start of Yuen Tsuen Ancient Trail**, on the edge of Tai Lam Country Park. Continue along in the direction of Tin Fu Tsai for 800 metres, passing close to the summit of **Shek Lung Kung** (石龍拱 Stone Dragon Arch).

Look south for a view of the multiple levels of roads criss-crossing **Tsing Yi Island** and the 1377-metre span of Tsing Ma Bridge (once the world's longest road-and-rail suspension bridge) over Ma Wan Channel.

Follow the path through what used to be farmland but now looks like primeval forest, arriving at a concrete road in just over 2km. Turn left, away from a bridge, then 750 metres later go right, up the steps signed Tin Fu Tsai campsite. Follow this excellent path for 400 metres, then cross a river via Tin Tsing Bridge leading to **Tin Fu Tsai campsite** 田夫仔營地. (Tin Fu Tsai village used to be the halfway point along the ancient trail, an important stopover.)

Go through the campsite to a concrete road and turn left. ▸ About 300 metres later turn left onto a footpath, then cross a bridge over the delightful **Lotus Stream** and reach a concrete road in about 1km. Turn right (W) signed Yuen Tsuen Ancient Trail and Tsing Lung Tau, then 400 metres later take steps down on the left, now following signs for Yuen Tsuen Ancient Trail and Tai Lam Chung Reservoir.

This is MacLehose Trail.

At a fork about 1km along, go right, heading up the valley (same signs), then the Yuen Tun Country Trail (Walk 2) joins from the left. Shortly afterwards, turn right, signed Tai Lam Chung Reservoir. ▸ Just over 1km along this almost jungle-like path, reach a concrete road and turn right, signed Ancient Trail.

Do not go straight ahead, which is Yuen Tun Country Trail, even though it is also signed for Tai Lam Chung Reservoir.

Cross a bridge 300 metres later, then turn left at a T-junction, signed Yuen Tsuen Ancient Trail and Tai Tong Shan Road bus stop. ▸ Follow the trail for 300 metres to the top of **Tai Lam Chung Reservoir**, then continue along the road as it curves right and upwards. ▸ In about 300 metres, turn right along a footpath signed Yuen Tsuen Ancient Trail. It joins with another 400-year-old path, the Nam Hang Pai Ancient Trail. Continue along, not taking any turnings, go past a typical Hong Kong **temple** dedicated to both Taoism and Buddhism, and later walk beside a beautiful **river**.

This is MacLehose Trail again.

The road is lined with sweet gum trees, which have beautiful red foliage in autumn.

Arrive at a fork about 2km later and go left, uphill, signed Tai Tong Road Bus Stop and Yuen Tsuen Ancient Trail, leading 150 metres later to a very infrequently used concrete road. Go left, uphill (no signs) for 600 metres, with views of Yuen Long Plain. ▸ Arrive at **Tai Tong barbecue area** 大棠燒烤場地. Turn right to walk along **Tai Tong Shan Road**, passing the **official end of Yuen Tsuen Ancient Trail** after 500 metres, at the border of Tai Lam Country Park. Continue walking for another 1km to a T-junction with **Kiu Hing Road**, with two cafés, and the bus stop is on the left on the opposite side of the road.

Yuen Long Plain is the biggest alluvial plain of the territory. Up to the 1960s it grew most of Hong Kong's rice.

# WALK 4
## *Ben Nevis*

| | |
|---|---|
| **Start** | Tam Shui Hang bus stop, Sha Tau Kok Road 担水坑巴士站, 沙頭角路 |
| **Finish** | Wo Hang bus stop, Sha Tau Kok Road 禾坑巴士站, 沙頭角路 |
| **Distance** | 8km |
| **Total ascent** | 600m |
| **Grade** | Difficult |
| **Time** | 4hr |
| **Terrain** | An unofficial, unmaintained route with some scrambling in places; steep up and down; mixture of dirt, stone and concrete paths |
| **Summits** | Yi Tung (439m), Sam Tung (392m), Ma Tseuk Leng (384m), Hung Fa Chai (Ben Nevis, 487m), Robin's Nest (492m) |
| **Map** | North East & Central New Territories |

On the pre-1957 admiralty chart, Hung Fa Chai is named Ben Nevis, after the highest mountain in the UK, so it was imperative to include it in this book! Check it out on the Hong Kong Historic Maps website: www.hkmaps.hk/mapviewer.html.

Only for the intrepid and adventurous, this unofficial, unsigned walk through shrubs and small trees on unmaintained but obvious paths is a delight, despite the chance that it may be overgrown in places. The reward is a view of two countries: a rural Hong Kong landscape of villages, fields and green hills contrasting with the skyscrapers of Shenzhen city.

Long trousers or leg protection are essential. If you are lucky, the path will have been marked with ribbons, but this cannot be relied upon. GPS is strongly advised, not only for navigational purposes but also because the walk is very close to the Frontier Closed Area (FCA) adjacent to the Chinese border. It is illegal to enter the FCA without a permit, even accidentally.

## Public transport

**Beginning:** From Fanling MTR station (East Rail line) exit A2, take bus 78K, direction Sha Tau Kok. (Caution: the same bus stop is used here for both directions.)

**End:** Take bus 78K, direction Sheung Shui, to Fanling MTR station.

From the bus stop, head E and take the second left after 150 metres onto **Shan Tsui Village Road**. The fence along here is the border into the Frontier Closed Area (FCA).

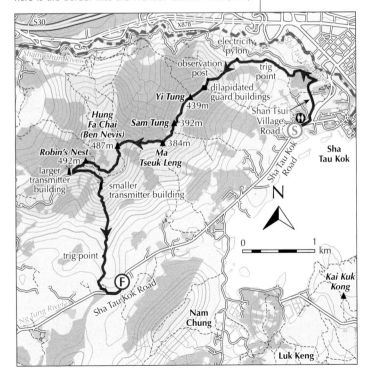

Turn left after 600 metres onto a good dirt path heading NW. Continue along for 850 metres, passing trenches and a pillbox left over from the Cold War, and arrive at a **trig point.**

After 500 metres, fork left and almost immediately walk beneath an **electricity pylon**. Fork left again after 200 metres, heading SW. Follow this rough stony path, which is very steep in places, and 350 metres later arrive at a ruinous **observation post**. Fork left and go behind the building, follow the railings, go past another pillbox and arrive 100 metres later at two **dilapidated guard buildings**. Do not follow the footpath through these unstable, dangerous-looking structures but instead go around them and follow the concrete path on the other side, which rapidly becomes a rough dirt path along the ridge.

As recently as 1987, the boundary to the **Frontier Closed Area** ran along the top of this ridge, complete with barbed wire fence. It is a testimony to decreased East–West tension that walking these Cold War relics is now allowed.

About 250 metres along is the summit of **Yi Tung** (二 峒 Second Hill, no marker). Walk thorough shade-giving greenery along the undulating ridge for 400 metres to the summit of **Sam Tung** (三峒 Third Hill, no marker). The path then opens up with a good view of the imposing route ahead. Descend steeply for 100 metres then continue along the ridge, arriving 300 metres later at **Ma Tseuk Leng** (no marker).

**Ma Tseuk Leng** 麻雀嶺 means Sparrow Ridge. Confusingly, Robin's Nest was also once called Ma Tseuk Leng because of the many birds there, and there is a village with the same name on the lower slopes of this peak. In Mandarin, sparrow is pronounced 'mah-jong', hence the name of the tile game – because the sound of playing the game resembles the chirping of the birds.

Veer right (NW), continuing along the lovely, sinuous, grass-covered ridge for 650 metres. Fork right and ascend a short distance to the summit of **Hung Fa Chai** (Ben Nevis).

> **Ben Nevis**, named after the highest mountain in the UK, is now officially called Hung Fa Chai 紅花寨, meaning Red Flower Fortress. Legend says (with some archaeological evidence) that a gang of Robin-Hood-like mountain thieves/government rebels built a mountain stronghold here in the Qing Dynasty.
>
> The summit, anticlimactically marked with just a single stone, is the most northerly of all Hong Kong's hills over 300 metres.

Head S from the summit for 200 metres, then veer right, heading SW. Nearly at the brow 200 metres further is a footpath crossroads; go right (N), uphill. About 100 metres later, go down a short distance, cross another path then immediately veer right, leading 150 metres later to the trig point at the summit of **Robin's Nest**. ▶

*A misty view of Pak Sin Leng Country Park from 'Ben Nevis'*

Robin's Nest in Chinese is Hung Fa Leng 紅花嶺, meaning Red Flower Ridge, because the profusion of azalea (*Rhododendron simsii Planch.*) turns the mountain bright red in spring.

*Descending through dense growth of iron fern*

Head SW to the **larger of two transmitter buildings**, which has a jeep road going to it. Get to the road but, instead of going along it, turn immediately left onto a path and follow the telegraph poles to the second, **smaller transmitter building** 500 metres along. Walk past it and take the rough path heading down. After 1.2km, reach a **trig point** (no name), continue the descent and arrive 200 metres later at a concrete path. Follow it to the right, down steps for 300 metres to a concrete road. Turn left, leading to **Sha Tau Kok Road**. Turn left again and the bus stop for Fanling MTR station is 250 metres further on the opposite side of the road.

# WALK 5
*Tung Ping Chau*

| | |
|---|---|
| **Start/Finish** | Tung Ping Chau Pier 東坪洲碼頭 |
| **Distance** | 7km |
| **Total ascent** | 140m |
| **Grade** | Easy |
| **Time** | 3hr |
| **Terrain** | A mixture of dirt, stone and concrete paths, plus beach and walking on rocks, with scrambling if exploring the rocky coastline |
| **Summits** | Hok Ngam Teng (45m) |
| **Map** | North East & Central New Territories |

Tung Ping Chau (meaning East Flat Island) is the easternmost island of Hong Kong. As in the Sharp Peak Walk (Walk 13), the boat ride is part of the adventure. The island is UNESCO-listed for its geology: the sedimentary rocks here are the youngest in all Hong Kong, and it is renowned for its fascinating rocky landscape, formed after years of weathering. There is no mains water or electricity on the island. It used to have a population of over 2000, but at the time of writing, in spring 2022, there is only one permanent resident, an old lady of 88 years.

The tree-shaded route circumnavigates the whole island, visiting deserted villages, amazing beaches and the rocky coastline. The waters around here are Hong Kong's fourth designated marine park, full of corals and wildlife. Due to the ferry times, there should be plenty of time to explore the intertidal rock pools filled with small fish, sea urchins and crabs. In summer, swimming, snorkelling and scuba-diving are popular activities, making it eminently suitable for a family day out. On ferry days, restaurants near the pier serve fresh local seafood.

To avoid walking alongside tour groups, who tend to go clockwise around the island, our route is anticlockwise. For safety reasons, check the tide times online before exploring the rocky coastline.

## Public transport

**Beginning:** From University MTR station (East Rail line) exit B, turn immediately left and follow the bicycle lane for 600 metres to its end. Turn left following signs for the pier, take the underpass, then go left for 400 metres to Ma Liu Shui Public Pier 馬尿水碼頭 for the *kaito* (街渡 small ferry). Important: from the underpass, do not turn right to Ma Liu Shui Pier 3. The ferry crossing takes 90min, weekends and public holidays only, one sailing per day: outbound 9am, return 5.15pm; see Appendix A.

Although mostly deserted and slowly crumbling, Tai Tong Village does have restaurants open on ferry days.

Walk off the pier and go right, along a huge beach, looking out for many examples of the famed sedimentary rock plus huge clumps of brain corals washed up after typhoons. Arrive 250 metres later at **Tai Tong Village** 大塘村. ◀ Continue along the main path that circumnavigates the island for another 700 metres to the second ruined village, **Chau Mei** (洲尾 Island Tail). At the end of the concrete path, continue in the same direction on the beach, then walk along the rocky shore.

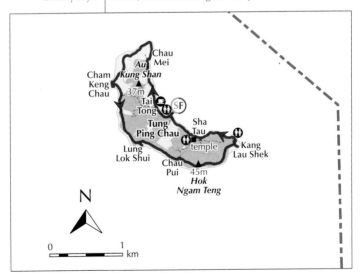

The **iron-rich rock** along here has weathered and dissolved, leaving a lace-like filigree pattern, almost as if rusted away. This part of the route may be difficult during high tide, and the rocks will be very slippery if wet.

Reach the concrete path again and follow it, signed Cham Keng Chau. About 800 metres further, arrive at **Cham Keng Chau** (斬頸洲 Chopped Neck Island), a sea stack now separated from the main island by erosion. If the tide permits, walk down the natural steps, through the gap separating the stack from the island, and explore these fascinating rocks, with their stromatolites, goose barnacles and rock pools. Retrace your steps to the main route, now following signs for Lung Lok Shui. Ignore a left turn (which is a shortcut back to the pier), and continue for about 1km to arrive at **Lung Lok Shui** 龍落水.

*Cham Keng Chau*

**Lung Lok Shui** means Dragon Diving into the Sea. It is a layer of tough white chert with serrated ridges, needing very little imagination to see it as a dragon's back. Chert is of biological origin, the petrified remains of siliceous ooze, the silt and algae-rich sediment that covers the ocean floor. Composed of quartz crystals, it is a hard fine-grained rock, highly resistant to weathering, which explains why it stands proud of the surrounding softer rock. The stones to the west are known as Lung Lun Tsui, meaning Dragon's Scales.

After exploration, return to the main route and continue to follow it SE, now following signs for Kang Lau Shek. Along here there are several paths down to the fascinating rock structures: clamber down only when it is

*Kang Lau Shek*

*Hong Kong Harbour*

safe to do so and the tide allows. Also along this stretch is the truly conch-shaped Conch Cave, which is only accessible at exceptionally low tide.

About 600 metres further, arrive at **Chau Pui** (洲背 Island Back). ▶ Continue along the coast (still signed Kang Lau Shek) for another 600 metres to the summit of **Hok Ngam Teng** (鶴岩頂 Crane Granite Top): marked by a solstice indicator, this is the highest point of the island at a massive 45m!

Follow the path for another 500 metres to arrive at **Kang Lau Shek** (更樓石 Watchman's Tower Rock), two huge two-storey blocks of stone that have resisted weathering, surrounded by numerous rock pools. After exploration, return to the route, then 60 metres later arrive at a beach. Walk along for 600 metres to the ruins of **Sha Tau** village 沙頭村. ▶ After 200 metres, the concrete path restarts, leading 500 metres later back to the **pier**.

There is a turning on the left here, a shortcut to the pier through four old villages.

Here is a Tin Hau temple, built in 1765, dedicated to the Chinese Sea Goddess Tin Hau or Mazu (see Walk 14).

# WALK 6
*Hanging Lantern and the ghost villages*

| | |
|---|---|
| **Start** | Wu Kau Tang minibus terminus, Chi Sum Road 烏蛟騰小巴站, 祠心路 |
| **Alternative start/finish** | Lai Chi Wo Pier 荔枝窩碼頭 |
| **Finish** | Luk Keng Road–Bride's Pool Road minibus terminus, Luk Keng 鹿頸路新娘潭路小巴站, 鹿頸 |
| **Distance** | 17km (first half: 7.75km; first half short: 7.25km; second half: 9km) |
| **Total ascent** | 810m (first half: 420m; first half short: 200m; second half: 390m) |
| **Grade** | Difficult (first half: difficult; first half short: easy; second half: easy) |
| **Time** | 6hr 15min (first half: 3hr 15min; first half short: 2hr 15min; second half: 3hr) |
| **Terrain** | A mixture of dirt, stone and concrete paths, plus scrambling up and down Tiu Tang Lung summit |
| **Summits** | Tiu Tang Lung (Hanging Lantern, 416m) |
| **Map** | North East & Central New Territories |

Tiu Tang Lung (吊燈籠 Hanging Lantern) is a challenging summit with rewarding panoramic views, including ethereal misty islands on a motionless calm sea. The route takes you along ancient ways, through a time capsule of once flourishing Hakka villages, now mostly deserted and becoming 'ghost villages'. Lai Chi Wo is one of the still thriving villages, providing a glimpse into the lives of the Hakka people. This walk is incredibly green and quiet, with enormous numbers of mangroves, and finishes with an easy stroll along the shore, quite literally on the border with China.

To make this interesting walk more suitable for families, it could be done in two halves using the alternative start/finish at Lai Chi Wo Pier. The first half would start at Wu Kau Tang and finish at the pier, and could be further shortened by omitting Tiu Tang Lung summit. The second half would start at the pier and finish at Luk Keng.

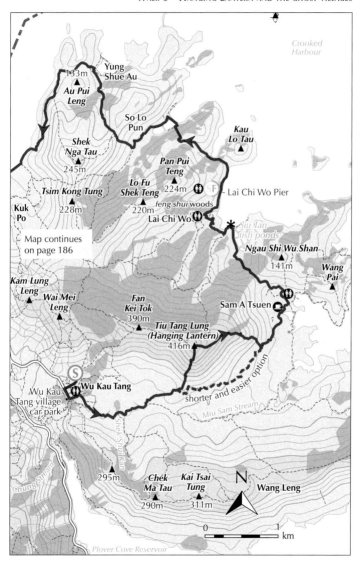

Crooked
Harbour

133m
▲
*Au Pui
Leng*

Yung
Shue Au

So Lo
Pun

*Shek
Nga Tau*
245m

*Kau
Lo Tau*
▲

*Pan Pui
Teng*
224m ▲

*Lo Fu
Shek Teng*
220m ▲

*feng shui woods*

Lai Chi Wo Pier

*Tsim Kong Tung*
228m ▲

*Kuk
Po*

Lai Chi Wo

Map continues
on page 186

*Ngau Shi Wu Shan*
141m ▲

Siu Tan
fish ponds

*Wang
Pai*

*Kam Lung
Leng*
▲

*Wai Mei
Leng*
▲

*Fan
Kei Tok*
390m ▲

*Tiu Tang Lung
(Hanging Lantern)*
416m ▲

Sam A Tsuen

S

*Wu Kau Tang*

Wu Kau
Tang village
car park

shorter and easier option

Miu Sam Stream

Shek Shui Kan

Chung Stream

295m
▲

*Chek
Ma Tau*
290m ▲

*Kai Tsai
Tung*
311m ▲

N

*Wang Leng*

0          1
          km

Plover Cove Reservoir

## Public transport

**Beginning:** From Tai Po Market MTR station (East Rail line) exit A3, take the underpass and turn left for the minibus station. Take green minibus 20R (hourly in the early morning, then every 1hr 30min; very busy, especially at weekends; see Appendix A). Alternatively, take bus 275R from Tai Po Market MTR station to Wu Tau Kang village car park (Sundays and public holidays only, every 15–20min).

**End:** Take green minibus 56K to Fanling MTR station (East Rail line).

**Alternative start/finish:** Take the ferry to/from Ma Liu Shui Pier (15min walk from University MTR station; see Walk 5, Public transport). The ferry operates on Sundays and public holidays only, 9am departure and 3.30pm return; see Appendix A.

Bus 275R terminus is here.

From the minibus stop, walk back (SW) for 200 metres to the end of Chi Sum Road, then turn left onto Wu Kau Tang Road. Arrive at **Wu Kau Tang village car park** after 150 metres. ◀ Go straight ahead onto a footpath by a shelter, down the steps, then across a bridge. Reach a T-junction and turn left to head E along a concrete path. Take the first right-hand footpath 150 metres later, signed Kau Tam Tso.

Walk along by the river, shaded by astounding clumps of giant bamboo. Keep following the main path (ignore any turnings) for 1.2km, then fork left up steps signed Lai Tau Shek (also signed Sam A Tsuen). About 600 metres along, reach a left turn up an unmarked, overgrown trail with a warning sign saying 'only for experienced and well-equipped hikers'. ◀ Turn left here to ascend to the summit of Tiu Tang Lung (Hanging Lantern).

See 'Tips on walking in Hong Kong' in the Introduction.

### Shorter and easier option
Ignore the turn for the ascent of Tiu Tang Lung, go straight ahead and follow the main path for 1.6km, where there is a turning on the left. This is where the descent from Tiu Tang Lung summit rejoins the shorter option.

## Main route

After turning left at the warning sign, reach an electricity pole 50 metres later, fork left and ascend for 650 metres. Initially this takes you through a shrubby tunnel of aromatic foliage, followed by more open terrain, then some scrambling to arrive at the summit of **Tiu Tang Lung**. From here there are great views of Double Haven Bay, with its well-known peaceful scenery of islands in the calm seas (living up to its English name) and deep-red rocks, rich in iron oxide, and of Pat Sin Leng mountain range (Wilson Trail, Section 9).

Take the rightmost (NE) path down, and fork right 50 metres later. Continue the difficult descent over steep and uneven terrain for just over 1km back to the main path, then turn left. ▶

Walk NE for 800 metres to **Sam A Tsuen** 三椏村. (This tiny place nestled in mangroves has a restaurant famed for bean curd dessert. Most restaurants here only open weekends/public holidays.) About 150 metres later, turn left at a crossroads, signed Lai Chi Wo. Walk through disused paddy fields, flat with irrigation channels, for

*View of Double Haven Bay from 'Hanging Lantern'*

The shorter option rejoins the route here.

## THE HAKKA

The Hakka are a subgroup of Chinese people who speak the Hakka dialect. Thought to originate from the north, they then settled in southern China and arrived in this area in the 1600s. They flourished as farmers and labourers in rural area until the 1960s, when the younger generation, being better educated, started to work in urban areas and some migrated abroad to Britain. Over the years, the remaining residents have stopped farming rice and bananas and moved to the city, leaving some villages with just a handful of elderly people while others are completely abandoned.

Under a revival scheme to promote sustainable village life, Lai Chi Wo is now a thriving community with school and temple both in use. It is a typical Hakka walled village with individual buildings arranged in a nine-by-three grid, plus *feng shui* woods behind the houses, believed to provide protection from disaster and bring good fortune.

There is a viewpoint a short way along on the left with views of Siu Tan fish ponds, extensive mangrove swamps and a huge container port across the water in China.

This is the alternative start/finish.

150 metres then go right at a fork (although both options go to the same place).

Continue along the main path (still signed Lai Chi Wo), pass a couple more restaurants, arrive at the coast 1.5km later and turn left. ◄ About 300 metres along, go right at a junction (same sign), pass a mangrove boardwalk, and 500 metres further arrive at **Lai Chi Wo** (荔枝窩 Lychee Nest, once famous for its lychee trees). Cross the bridge to the village square by the temple and turn right, signed Pier. Arrive at the **pier** 400 metres later. ◄

Walk along the shore for 300 metres, then follow the path inland; this is the ancient way between the isolated villages of this area. After a small ascent and descent, cross a long concrete walkway over an estuary 1km later. At its far end, turn left, signed **So Lo Pun** 鎖羅盆, which you reach 600 metres later.

The abandoned and mysterious village of **So Lo Pun** is the focus of many Bermuda-Triangle-like myths, such as all the inhabitants having inexplicably vanished overnight, or died in a boat accident on the way to a wedding banquet. Even the name

is enigmatic: it literally means 'locked compass', because allegedly all compasses fail here.

The truth of the abandonment is simply that people left to seek better opportunities when the prices of their farming produce crashed in the 1970s. However, the graves are still maintained and former residents attend government meetings about redeveloping this area. Although the buildings are dilapidated, there is evidence of ownership, and visitors may notice newly hung antithetical couplets at the front door of the houses – these pairs of hanging scrolls are inscribed with lines of poems expressing happiness, well wishes or tales of heroic actions.

About 250 metres after the village, fork right, signed Luk Keng and Yung Shue Au. Follow this for 1.2km, along spectacularly beautiful, ruinous ancient ways to **Yung Shue Au** 榕樹凹. Go through the ruins of this abandoned village, cross over a crossroads within the village, and then at a junction towards the end of the village fork left, signed Luk Keng. Follow this path for 2km, mostly following the shoreline of **Starling Inlet** 沙頭角海,

*Huge amount of mangroves in the estuary*

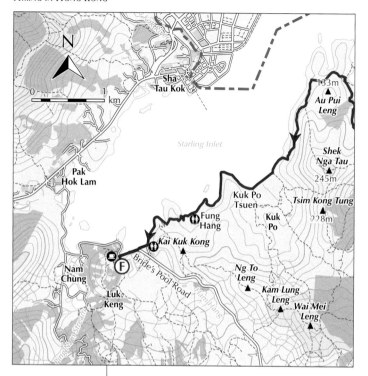

This path along Starling Inlet is the boundary of the Frontier Closed Area, with views of mainland China just across the water.

thereafter walking on an easy concrete path along the water's edge. ◄

Pass through **Kuk Po Tsuen** 谷埔村 and walk along a concrete walkway across an estuary filled with huge amounts of mangroves, followed by another walkway with the village of **Fung Hang** 鳳坑 to your left. After 2km of easy walking, go up the last short ascent then about 1km later reach some houses. Continue along the coast a short way to **Bride's Pool Road** and turn right (W). The end of the walk is 300 metres further, with cafés, restaurants, shops and the minibus stop on the left, immediately after the bridge.

# WALK 7
*Wong Leng and Bride's Pool*

| | |
|---|---|
| **Start** | Sze Tau Leng Tsuen minibus terminus 獅頭嶺村小巴站 |
| **Finish** | Wu Kau Tang minibus terminus, Chi Sum Road 烏蛟騰小巴站, 祠心路 |
| **Distance** | 10.5km |
| **Total ascent** | 780m |
| **Grade** | Difficult |
| **Time** | 4hr 30min |
| **Terrain** | A mixture of stone and concrete steps, dirt, stone and concrete paths, plus road and pavement; some steep and uneven slopes, with scrambling on the optional summit only |
| **Summits** | Wong Leng (639m); optional: Kwai Tau Leng (486m) |
| **Map** | North East & Central New Territories |

Pat Sin Leng Country Park is one of the prettiest and most remote country parks in Hong Kong. Section 9 of Wilson Trail traverses the entire mountain range of Pat Sin Leng (Eight Immortals Ridge), but this route starts at a much lower level along Nam Chung Country Trail, quaint yet equally beautiful. It then ascends to the ridge to get a taste of the majestic mountain range before descending via mossy green paths, crossing over to the legendary Bride's Pool area. The Bride's Pool Waterfall, Bride's Pool and Mirror Pool are well known to all Hongkongers, an all-time favourite location for family outings, with beautiful scenery and a natural freshwater swimming pool.

There is also an optional extra summit, providing 360-degree views of a rural Hong Kong landscape in contrast to the skyscrapers of Shenzhen in mainland China.

## Public transport

**Beginning:** From Fanling MTR station (East Rail line) exit C, take green minibus 56B. (The front of the minibus says Tan Chuk Hang, but it goes further to the required terminus at Sze Tau Leng Tsuen.)

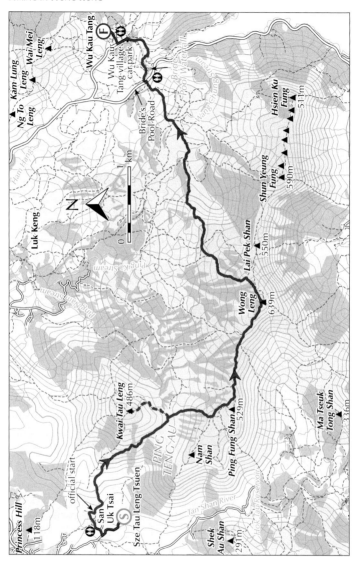

*The path up to Pat Sin Leng with Kwai Tau Leng in the background*

**End:** Take green minibus 20R to Tai Po Market MTR station (East Rail line) 大埔墟港鐵站 (every 1hr to 1hr 30min; very busy, especially at weekends; see Appendix A). Alternatively, take bus 275R from Wu Tau Kang village car park (near the end of the walk) to Tai Po Market MTR station (Sundays and public holidays only, every 15–20min).

From the minibus stop, walk back along the road heading NW, past a pavilion, then 400 metres later take the first right turn, signed San Uk Tsai 新屋仔. Continue on the road through **San Uk Tsai** village for about 500 metres, past the **toilets**, to the **official start of Nam Chung Country Trail** 南涌郊遊徑 with some steps on the left.

Go up this trail for 1.5km; the way is shaded, green and tree-lined, with cycad ferns (*Brainea insignis*) beneath. The path levels off, then the terrain becomes more open at **Ping Teng Au** (平頂坳 Flat Top Pass); to the right there are magnificent views of the ridge from Ping Fung Shan to Pat Sin Leng. About 500 metres further, arrive at the first junction on the trail. To continue the trail, go right (SE), signed Pat Sin Range. Alternatively, there is an optional extra here to Kwai Tau Leng.

189

### Optional summit: Kwai Tau Leng

This adds 1.5km, 150m ascent and 1hr. Go straight ahead at the junction, signed Nam Chung, and 500 metres later go up an unmaintained (may be overgrown) unsigned path on the left. (If you reach distance post C2506, you have missed the turning.) Ascend for 300 metres, with minimal scrambling, to the summit of **Kwai Tau Leng** (龜頭嶺 Tortoise Head Ridge). From here, there are great views of Ben Nevis (Walk 4) and the mainland Chinese town of Shenzhen sprawling beneath a tall white tower on a mountaintop. Retrace your steps to the junction on the main trail.

This is Wilson Trail, Section 9. The unusual white stone of the path is calcareous siltstone, laid down in the Carboniferous era 300 million years ago.

Head SE from the junction, signed Pat Sin Range, on an enjoyable ascent for 1km (ignoring any turnings) to a footpath crossroads beneath **Ping Fung Shan**; turn left, signed Pat Sin Leng. ◄ This leads to a long, simply stunning ridge, showing just how rural and green Hong Kong can be.

After about 1.7km, reach a sign saying **Wong Leng**. Take the path behind it for a short distance to the summit (the 15th highest in Hong Kong), marked with a trig point. Return to the sign and continue the ridge walk, enjoying amazing views: ahead is Wilson Trail, snaking fantastically onwards, and to the right is Plover Cove (Walk 8) and the 76m-tall statue of the Bodhisattva.

On the descent, look south-west for views of Lai Pek Shan and the eight summits of Pat Sin Leng, from Shun Yeung Fung to Hsien Ku Fung.

After about 150 metres, turn off Wilson Trail and go left, downwards, signed Luk Keng and Nam Chung. ◄ Fork left 200 metres later (same signs); then 1km further, at the bottom, turn right at a T-junction (no sign, but there is one of Hong Kong's overcautious notices saying 'for experienced walkers only'). The path ahead is rocky and uneven but only slightly challenging; walk along with views entirely of greenery – not a tower block in sight.

Cross over Wilson Trail 1.5km later, now following signs for Bride's Pool. Continue along a beautiful stone-built track next to a river for 600 metres to a T-junction with another path. Turn left downhill (same sign) and 750 metres later arrive at **Bride's Pool Road**. Cross over the road onto Bride's Pool Nature Trail, which is slightly to the left.

Cross the bridge over a lovely river then turn right, signed Chung Mei and Wu Kau Tang. **Bride's Pool Waterfall** 新娘潭瀑布 is audible to the right. Turn right again after about 800 metres and cross over the granite bridge (built in 1906), following signs for Chung Mei. ▶ Just 50 metres along, turn left up the steps signed Wu Kau Tang and continue to zigzag up for 100 metres. Take the first left (same sign). About 400 metres later, cross a bridge over a river, then go up the slope to a shelter. This is **Wu Kau Tang village car park**. ▶ Continue along this road for 120 metres, turn right along Chi Sum Road, and the minibus terminus is 200 metres along at the end of this road.

According to the legend of **Bride's Pool Waterfall**, a bride was being carried to her wedding in a palanquin. Crossing a bridge over the pool, the porters slipped, she fell into the water and drowned. The pool was then named after her.

There are many unofficial small paths to explore in this area, going to Bride's Pool, Bride's Pool Waterfall, Mirror Pool and various viewpoints. Caution: the paths to these places can be slippery and there are drops with no safety barriers.

This is the ancient trail which used to link Wu Kau Tang with Chung Mei. There is a picnic area here.

Bus 275R leaves from here.

*Bride's Pool*

# WALK 8
*Plover Cove Reservoir Country Trail*

| | |
|---|---|
| **Start** | Wu Kau Tang minibus terminus, Chi Sum Road 烏蛟騰小巴站, 祠心路 |
| **Finish** | Tai Mei Tuk bus terminus 大美督巴士總站 |
| **Distance** | 18.5km |
| **Total ascent** | 780m |
| **Grade** | Difficult |
| **Time** | 6hr 30min |
| **Terrain** | A mixture of stone and concrete steps, pavement, dirt and concrete paths, and across three dams |
| **Summits** | Ma Tau Fung (295m), Kai Tsai Tung (311m), Tai Tung (295m), Mount Newland (303m), Luk Wu Tung (280m), Fu Tau Sha (110m), Cheung Pai Tun (125m) |
| **Map** | North East & Central New Territories |

This is a relatively new country trail around the largest reservoir in Hong Kong, which (amazingly) stores fresh water in the sea. The initial ascent leads high up to commanding views, followed by a giant ridge walk. Although there are no big mountains, the path undulates over many summits, getting progressively lower as it nears the water's edge, and finishes by crossing three dams.

This fabulous long walk is an astoundingly beautiful, peaceful route, with splendid views of Pat Sin Leng mountain range (Wilson Trail, Section 9), Double Haven Bay and its iron-rich red rocks, Ma On Shan and Sharp Peak in Sai Kung to the south, and across the water all the way to the east side of the New Territories.

There is almost no shade on the route, so you may wish to avoid doing it on the hottest of days.

**Public transport**

**Beginning:** From Tai Po Market MTR station (East Rail line) exit A3, take the underpass and turn left for the minibus station. Take green minibus 20R (hourly early morning, then every 1hr 30min; very busy, especially at weekends; see Appendix A). Alternatively, take bus 275R from Tai Po Market MTR station to Wu Tau Kang village car park (Sundays and public holidays only, every 15–20min).

**End:** Take bus 75K or green minibus 20C to Tai Po Market MTR station.

From the minibus stop, walk back (SW) for 200 metres to the end of Chi Sum Road, then turn left onto Wu Kau Tang Road. Arrive at **Wu Kau Tang village car park** after 150 metres. ▶ Go straight ahead onto a footpath by a shelter, down the steps, then across a bridge. Reach a T-junction, turn right and 50 metres later is the **official start**. There is a warning sign ('only for fit experienced well-equipped hikers'), and there are more warning signs further along. ▶

Turn left up the steps, initially along a path made entirely of roots. After 1.3km arrive at **Ma Tau Fung** (馬頭峰 Horse Head Peak), where there are great views of Wong Leng (Walk 7), Ben Nevis (Walk 4) and Tiu Tang Lung (Walk 6). Continue along the ridge path, now signed Luk Wu Tung, and 1.5km along reach the trig point of **Kai Tsai Tung** (雞仔峒 Chick Hill). After 500 metres, arrive at a T-junction at **Wang Leng Au** (橫嶺坳 Horizontal Ridge Pass) and turn right (same sign). This leads after 1.4km to the summit of **Tai Tung** 大峒 (meaning Big Mountain, despite it being only 295m high), marked by a wooden route sign. Turn right at the T-junction here, still following signs for Luk Wu Tung. ▶ Follow the path for 1.2km to **Mount Newland** 觀音峒.

The Chinese name for **Mount Newland** is Kwun Yam Tung, meaning Goddess of Mercy Mountain. Look back to see the amazing ridge and clifftop the route has just traversed.

Look out for the **red stones** beneath your feet; the colour is from already oxidised iron in the existing rock being further oxidised by volcanic processes. On the nearby coast the redness is even more striking, reflected in that place's name, Hung Shek Mun 紅石門, meaning Red Rocky Gateway.

Bus 275R terminus is here.

The route is graded difficult due to its length, not because of any technical difficulty. See 'Tips on walking in Hong Kong' in the Introduction.

The left turn here is the last opportunity to leave the trail to return to Wu Kau Tang if conditions become unfavourable.

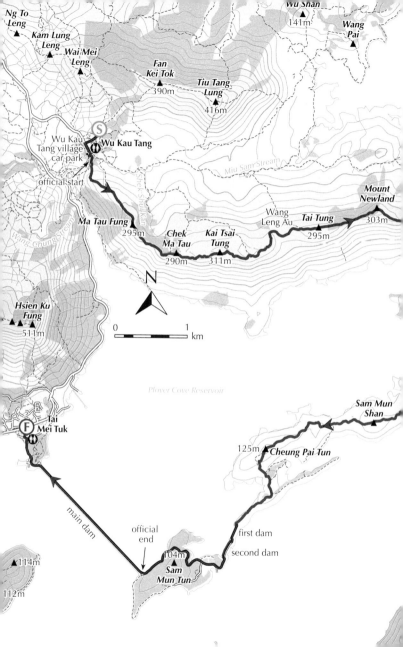

Double Haven

Luk Wu Tung
280m   295m

Ngor Kai Teng

Fu Tau Sha
110m

Kai Ma Tung
180m   207m
Shek Nga Tau

Continue along this wonderful ridge for another 1.7 km to **Luk Wu Tung** (鹿湖峒 Deer Lake Mountain), marked by a wooden route sign. Turn right down a lot of steps, signed Tai Mei Tuk. Next, along a lower but equally glorious ridge, arrive just over 2km further at **Fu Tau Sha** (虎頭沙 Tiger Head Sand). ▶

Continue for nearly 3km to **Cheung Pai Tun** (長牌墩 Long Plaque Mound), and then a further 1.5km to arrive at the **first dam**. Walk across it, then follow the road to a gate and turn right up the steps to the **second dam** (no signs). Cross it and walk down the steps to the left at the other end, then continue on the road. Follow it for 1.6km, go through a gate (it is to stop bikes, not walkers) to the **official end** of the trail just before the **main dam**. ▶

The views of the cliffs you were walking on earlier are even more dramatic from this angle.

The entire walk, circumnavigating the reservoir, can be appraised from the dam. Here is also the best viewpoint for the many peaks of Pat Sin Leng Country Park.

*The reservoir in its entirety from Luk Wu Tung*

195

*Walking between the freshwater reservoir and the deep blue sea*

Walk across the 2km-long dam, then follow the road for 250 metres to a roundabout and go straight ahead. Follow the pedestrian way beside the road for 400 metres, and the **Tai Mei Tuk** bus terminus is behind the public toilets.

## PLOVER COVE RESERVOIR

Does it seem illogical to store fresh water in the sea? This is what they have done at Plover Cove Reservoir, the largest reservoir in Hong Kong. Begun in 1960 and taking eight years to build, it stores 170 billion litres. This was the world's first coastal freshwater lake, made by damming the ocean in three places and pumping the seawater out. The main dam was the world's longest at the time it was built.

# WALK 9
## *Tai Po Kau Nature Reserve*

| | |
|---|---|
| **Start/Finish** | Chung Tsai Yuen bus stop, Tai Po Road 松仔園巴士站, 大埔道 |
| **Distance** | 10.5km |
| **Total ascent** | 660m |
| **Grade** | Easy |
| **Time** | 4hr |
| **Terrain** | A mixture of stone and concrete steps, road and pavement, and dirt, stone and concrete paths |
| **Map** | North East & Central New Territories |

With 460 hectares of subtropical forest and native species, Tai Po Kau Nature Reserve is a good example of post-war reforestation in Hong Kong. If you're lucky, you could spot a pangolin or a civet cat, but otherwise just enjoy the peaceful greenery of this well-maintained nature reserve, one of the premier bird-spotting places in Hong Kong.

This route is a combination of the reserve's excellent red, blue, yellow and brown walks, giving a flavour of each. They are all at different levels, with varying populations of plants and birds. Despite the ascent, it is easy walking and completely in shade, and the paths and navigation are superb, making it very suitable for families. This is not a mountainous route, but rather its appeal is in its nature and biodiversity.

## Public transport
**Beginning:** From Tai Wai MTR station (East Rail line) exit C, turn left and then left again (3min walk) to Tai Wai bus terminus 大圍鐵路站巴士總站. Take bus 72A.

**End:** Take bus 72A to Tai Wai bus terminus and walk to the MTR station.

From the bus stop, go W for 50 metres towards **Tai Po Kau Garden** 大埔滘花園. Turn left just before the garden and

197

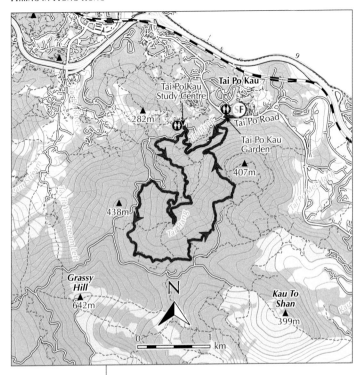

Tai Po Kau Study
Centre used to be a
village, then became
an experimental
farm. There is a
pretty garden and a
stream, with many
different birds around
the bird feeders.

go through the nature reserve entrance. Go up the steep road for about 750 metres, then fork right, staying on the road signed **Tai Po Kau Study Centre**, which you reach 250 metres later. ◄

Continue along the road for 800 metres then take a downward footpath on the left, which is the red walk. Follow this walk, lined with spectacular ferns and rattans, and go left at a fork 1.5km later. After 100 metres, cross a pretty bridge over a river and go right, up the steps, now following the blue walk.

Follow this upstream for 700 metres, cross a bridge on the right, then turn right to head downstream. About 500 metres later, take the first turning on the left to continue the blue walk, then 100 metres along fork left upwards, now following the yellow and brown walks.

Ignoring any turnings for 2.7km, continue through the lush green forest, admiring birds, butterflies, and crayfish in the brook, and crossing rivers over charming stepping stones or bridges. At a toilet sign, go straight ahead to stay on the brown trail (the yellow walk is to the right). Continue for about 1.5km, until the brown trail is rejoined by the yellow walk. Follow them for 1km to a T-junction with the Tai Po Kau Nature Trail and turn right to follow it (against the direction of the arrows) for 750 metres. Reach a concrete road, turn right, downhill, and retrace your steps to the beginning. Cross the road for the return bus stop.

> **Tai Po Kau Nature Reserve** is, by design, the most natural place in Hong Kong. The aim is to recreate a primeval subtropical forest with native trees, and countless examples of more than 100 different species of trees have been planted since 1926. This was the first place in Hong Kong to begin reforestation after the depredations of World War 2.

*Sun-dappled ferns on the forest floor*

# WALK 10
## *Lion Rock and the walk of many hills*

| | |
|---|---|
| **Start** | Choi Hung MTR station (Kwun Tong line) exit B 彩虹港鐵站 |
| **Finish** | Lok Fu MTR station (Kwun Tong line) 樂富港鐵站 |
| **Distance** | 11.75km |
| **Total ascent** | 1080m |
| **Grade** | Challenging |
| **Time** | 6hr |
| **Terrain** | Mostly footpaths and steps, including rough paths plus some scrambling up to Kowloon Peak |
| **Summits** | Kowloon Peak (602m), Middle Hill (585m), Tung Shan (544m), Lion Rock (495m), and many unnamed peaks |
| **Map** | North East & Central New Territories |

Beginning literally from the door of an MTR station, this unofficial hence unsigned route incorporates a simply fabulous ridge walk, with views gazing down onto the bustling centre of Kowloon, overlooking the New Territories, and south to the northern shore of Hong Kong Island just beyond the harbour.

Kowloon (九龍 Nine Dragons) refers to eight mountains and a Song Dynasty emperor. This route to Lion Rock is recommended since it takes in many other peaks including six out of the eight 'dragons'! You are guaranteed a massive sense of achievement at the end.

GPS would be advantageous but is not essential. Beware: fatalities have occurred on the climb to Lion Rock (head), so this is not included in our route; caution is also recommended on the ascent to Kowloon Peak as there are steep drops nearby, although not on our route.

From the MTR exit, walk straight ahead (E) along Clear Water Bay Road, then turn left 150 metres along, just before the **Ngau Chi Wan freshwater pumping station**, onto a pedestrianised path. Turn right up the steps in less than 100 metres. At the top of the steps (ignoring any turnings), keep to the left of Pak Fung House (a block of

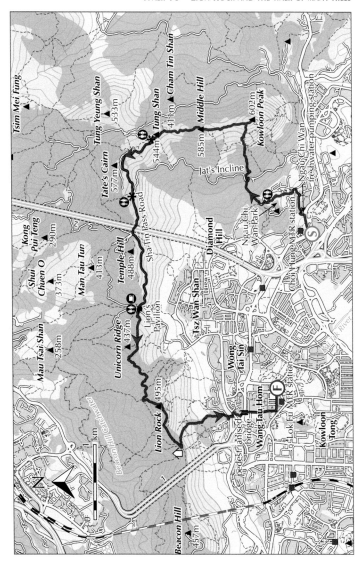

Tsim Mei Fung ▲

Cham Tin Shan ▲

Tung Yeung Shan
533m

Tung Shan
411m ▲ Middle Hill

Tung Shan
544m

Kowloon Peak
602m

Ngau Chi Wan
freshwater-pumping-station ▲

Tate's Cairn
577m

Jat's Incline

585m

Sha Tin Pass Road

Ngau Chi Wan Park ▲

Kong Pui Teng
290m

Shui Chuen O
373m

Man Tau Tun
413m

Temple Hill
488m

Diamond Hill

Mau Tsai Shan
258m

Unicorn Ridge
437m

Lion's Pavilion

Tsz Wan Shan

Choi Hung MTR Station

S

Wong Tai Sin

Lion Rock
495m

Wong Tai Hom

Pedestrianised bridge

F

Kowloon Tong

Lok Fu MTR Station

Kowloon Tong

Beacon Hill Catchwater

km

Beacon Hill
457m

N

*The squatter dwellings under Lion Rock have become modern residential tower blocks*

flats) on a quiet road, then 200 metres later, just before Choi Wan Community Centre Home Affairs Department, take a left-hand turn, going up the first set of stairs. At the top, turn left, cross the road and go into **Ngau Chi Wan Park 牛池灣公園**.

## NGAU CHI WAN

The name Ngau Chi Wan, meaning Buffalo Pool Bay, dates from the Ming Dynasty. The Hakka villagers (Walk 6) named the place after a big pool shaped like a buffalo crouching over the water. In the 1600s, the villagers were predominantly paddy farmers, but after World War 2 they became fishermen and sailors, and the land was used to grow more profitable vegetables.

In the 1970s, the site was used as landfill as part of reclamation around the bay, and farming was abandoned. By 2000, the Hong Kong government decided to regenerate the area, and this park was constructed to reflect on environmental values. This is a typical story of the land of Hong Kong.

Take any route uphill, heading N to the highest point of the park, then walk NE along the maintenance road behind the upper **toilet block**. Turn left up the steps through a pedestrian gate (before Fung Shing Street). Just 100 metres up, turn right at a pagoda-shaped shelter, following signs for Jat's Incline. At the top of the 572 steps, reach a road (**Jat's Incline**), turn right, downhill, then 50 metres later turn left (E) onto a footpath (initially through a picnic site).

Keep going up, past a shelter (with excellent views of Tate's Cairn and Lion Rock), for 200 metres to a T-junction with a non-potable water trough, and turn left (NE). Continue up the rough path through sub-tropical shrubs, with mild scrambling required at times. There are multiple paths closer to the top – simply head upwards. After about 750 metres, keep to the left of a big lump of rock. Reach a footpath crossroads 300 metres later, and turn right for **Kowloon Peak**. ▶ Return to the footpath crossroads.

This is the 18th highest peak in Hong Kong, also called Fei Ngo Shan 飛鵝山, meaning Flying Goose Hill. There is a heliport pad here and multiple transmission buildings.

Now take the path heading N along a ridge, go down a few steps, then veer left, staying above the electricity transformer. Continue for 600 metres along this interesting ridge walk, through deep bamboos. Arrive at **Middle Hill** (also called Cheung Shan 象山 Elephant Hill), then

*The dense bamboo-lined path after Kowloon Peak*

203

Both Wilson and MacLehose Trails join along here.

The military stones mark the former frontier between British colonial Hong Kong and China: see MacLehose Trail, Section 5.

*Sitting on Lion Rock body, looking at the head*

progress via some minor unnamed peaks. Walk beneath an electricity pylon, then after 800 metres reach a road at **Tung Shan** (東山 East Hill), with two Kowloon Peak **viewing points**. Turn left along Fei Ngo Shan Road, which later becomes **Sha Tin Pass Road**, heading W. ◄

Continue along this road for nearly 3km, go past the **Lion's Pavilion** 獅子亭 (a pagoda with two lion statues), then at a leftward hairpin bend, go up the steps on the right-hand side heading W into Lion Rock Country Park, signed Lion Rock. The top of the steps 500 metres later marks the beginning of **Unicorn Ridge** (雞胸山 Chicken Breast Hill). Walk along this path through light subtropical woodland with some shade, following signs for Beacon Hill. Continue for just over 1km, passing some military marker stones, then take a turning on the left for Lion Rock. ◄

Located between the New Territories and Kowloon, the three peaks of **Lion Rock** – head, body and rump – can be seen for miles around. Because of its central location, it is a popular hiking destination, especially for sunset and views of Hong Kong by night.

Many Hongkongers consider this iconic peak an emblem representing the 'never give up' spirit of the city. This stems from the 1970s TV soap *Below the Lion Rock*, reflecting life during that era through the eyes of several families living in squatter dwellings and council flats.

Arrive at **Lion Rock 獅子山** summit (rump) after a long set of steps (about 350 metres), then turn right to walk W along the ridge, passing Lion Rock (body). Continue along the path and go down the steps just before Lion Rock (head). Rejoin MacLehose Trail after 400 metres, head SE and arrive 150 metres later at a multiway junction with a **shelter**. Take the path signed Wang Tau Hom, which twists to head E. Follow this well-made path down for 1km and reach a road at the bottom of the steps.

Turn right then immediately left, continue on the road to go past a shelter, and shortly afterwards go down the first set of steps on the left, signed Chuk Yuen Road. Reach the road, cross it then take a ramp to the right of a bus shelter. Walk to the right of the tower blocks at the bottom and then head SE to cross a **pedestrianised bridge** over a main road. Take the stairs down to another estate, then go straight ahead along Fu Yue Street. Continue heading S as the road changes names and crosses other streets, then 500 metres later it bends left 90 degrees. **Lok Fu MTR station** is on the right after 100 metres.

# WALK 11
*Tai Tan and Cheung Sheung Country Trails*

| | |
|---|---|
| **Start** | Hoi Ha minibus terminus, Sai Kung 海下小巴總站, 西貢 |
| **Finish** | Shui Long Wo bus stop, Sai Sha Road 水浪窩巴士站, 西沙路 |
| **Alternative finish** | Hoi Ha Road, Sai Kung West Country Park 海下路, 西貢西郊野公園 |
| **Distance** | 16km (short version: 7km; MacLehose option: 16km) |
| **Total ascent** | 800m (short version: 390m; MacLehose option: 990m) |
| **Grade** | Moderate (short version: easy; MacLehose option: difficult) |
| **Time** | 5hr 30min (short version: 2hr 30min; MacLehose option: 6hr 30min) |
| **Terrain** | Easy shoreline dirt paths, with a short beach section; the second part is on dirt paths with a long descent down steps, finishing with easy walking by a catchwater; the optional extra to Wa Mei Shan is slightly steep and could be difficult if wet |
| **Summits** | Optional: Wa Mei Shan (391m) |
| **Map** | Sai Kung & Clear Water Bay |

This is a delightful walk joining two official trails. Tai Tan Country Trail is a lovely gentle coastal walk with sea views, suitable for families. Near the start is the Marine Life Centre, with exhibitions and glass-bottomed boat. The short version of Walk 11 ends at the finish point of Tai Tan Country Trail.

Cheung Sheung Country Trail includes a great ascent through amazing woodlands, plus an optional extra to the summit of Wa Mei Shan, which gives the best views. It ends with a long descent followed by exceptionally easy walking along a catchwater. For more of a challenge, leave the main route after visiting Wa Mei Shan and switch to the MacLehose option, which follows Section 3 of MacLehose Trail to its end at Sai Sha Road.

From the minibus stop, walk down the road into **Hoi Ha** village (no signs at beginning of walk). Follow the main path as it zigzags through the village and shops. After the

## Public transport

**Beginning:** From Choi Hung MTR station (Kwun Tong line) exit C2, take bus 92 to Sai Kung bus terminus 西貢巴士總站, then from the adjacent green minibus station, take green minibus 7.

**End:** Take bus 299X or 99 to Sai Kung bus terminus then bus 92 to Choi Hung MTR station.

**Alternative finish:** Take green minibus 7 to Sai Kung bus terminus then bus 92 to Choi Hung MTR station.

village, follow signs for Tai Tan and Wan Tsai, and reach a **limekiln** after 300 metres.

> The main source of income for **Hoi Ha** village from the early 20th century until World War 2 was producing lime from coral and seashells, for use in the building industry.
>
> Further along the route is the **Marine Life Centre** (open weekends, advance booking required, see Appendix A), which is a fascinating juxtaposition to the limekiln. This area is now part of the Hoi Ha Wan Marine Park, where all corals are protected.

Pass the **Marine Life Centre** 500 metres later, and continue along the lovely path for 800 metres through dense vegetation with intermittent views of the sea, which can be heard lapping the shore. Turn right, down steps signed Tai Tan, and continue for 1.5km with excellent views of Sharp Peak (Walk 13) across the water. Reach a junction and go left, signed Tai Tan Country Trail.

Continue along the undulating path parallel to the shoreline of **Long Harbour** for 1km, walk across the top of a small **beach**, then in 2km arrive at **Tai Tan** (大灘 Big Beach). The path becomes concrete; follow it for about 200 metres as it winds its way around some buildings, then take a set of steps on the right. ▶

No sign; if you get to a bridge, you have missed the steps.

Go past a house (No. 4, Tai Tan, Sai Kung), then up the steps right next to it, with signs shortly after you begin

*The route goes across a small beach*

For the alternative finish, stop here and take green minibus 7 on this side of the road (no bus stop, just flag it down).

This is also MacLehose Trail, Section 3. There is a shop here, open weekends only.

the ascent. Continue along this trail (ignore a right-hand turn 150 metres along) and reach **Hoi Ha Road** 1km from Tai Tan. This is the end of Tai Tan Country Trail. ◄

To continue the walk, turn left and 350 metres along on the right is the **official start of Cheung Sheung Country Trail**. Go up this wonderful trail, surrounded by massive trees. After 2.5km (ignoring a couple of turnings), arrive at a multiway junction at **Cheung Sheung campsite  嶂上 營地**. ◄ Head straight ahead (W) then 250 metres along is a fork: go right to stay on the main route, or left for an optional extra to Wa Mei Shan and the MacLehose option.

### Optional summit: Wa Mei Shan
The summit adds 1.5km, 60m ascent and 40min. At the fork, go left along MacLehose Trail, signed Shui Long Wo. About 600 metres later, at MacLehose **distance post M057**, take an unsigned, unmaintained track on the right, leading up to **Wa Mei Shan** summit (畫眉山 Draw Eyebrow Hill, no trig point). ◄ The views are absolutely astounding, the best in Sai Kung area: allow extra time to admire every peak of the entire eastern portion of the New Territories, a huge amount of MacLehose Trail, and much more.

Care may be needed on the slightly steep path, which could be slippery if wet.

Retrace your steps to MacLehose **distance post M057**. To complete Walk 11 via the main route, retrace

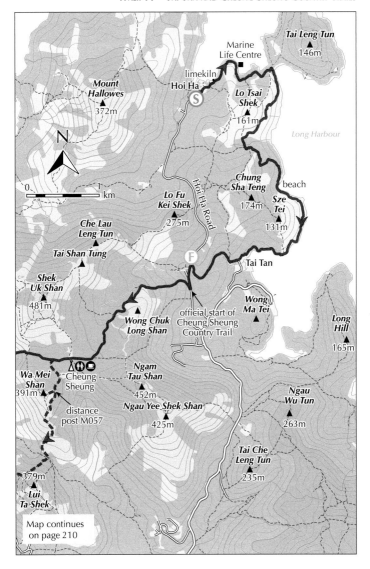

Marine
Life Centre

*Tai Leng Tun*
▲ 146m

limekiln

Hoi Ha
(S)

*Lo Tsai
Shek*
▲ 161m

*Long Harbour*

*Mount
Hallowes*
▲ 372m

N

*Chung
Sha Teng*
▲ 174m

beach

*Sze
Tei*
▲ 131m

0                    1
km

*Lo Fu
Kei Shek*
▲ 275m

*Che Lau
Leng Tun*
▲

Hoi Ha Road

*Tai Shan Tung*
▲

Tai Tan

*Shek
Uk Shan*
▲ 481m

*Wong Chuk
Long Shan*
▲

official start of
Cheung Sheung
Country Trail

*Wong
Ma Tei*
▲

*Long
Hill*
▲ 165m

△🏠🚻
Cheung
Sheung

*Ngam
Tau Shan*
▲ 452m

*Wa Mei
Shan*
▲ 391m

distance
post M057

*Ngau Yee Shek Shan*
▲ 425m

*Ngau
Wu Tun*
▲ 263m

*Tai Che
Leng Tun*
▲ 235m

▲ 379m

*Lui
Ta Shek*
▲

Map continues
on page 210

209

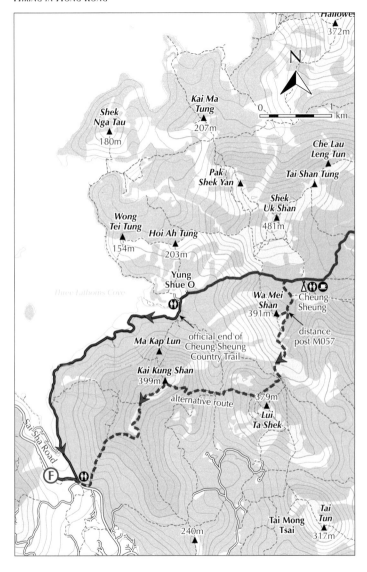

your steps to the fork near Cheung Sheung campsite; or for the MacLehose option, turn right.

**Alternative route: MacLehose option**
For a more challenging version of the main route: after descending from Wa Mei Shan, turn right at **distance post M057** and follow MacLehose Trail until it rejoins Walk 11 at **Sai Sha Road**. See MacLehose Trail, Section 3.

From the fork after Cheung Sheung campsite, go right to continue on the main route, following signs to Yung Shue O, then 350 metres later at a footpath crossroads go straight ahead (same sign). Next, descend along shaded green paths with many steps, hence the nickname Jacob's Ladder, for what feels like a long, long way but is only 1.2km. Arrive at **Yung Shue O Village**, turn left along the road and 500 metres along is the **official end of Cheung Sheung Country Trail**. However, with no public transport it is necessary to walk further.

Continue along the road (restricted access therefore very quiet), mostly by a catchwater for 4km (ignoring a right turn to Kei Ling Ha Lo Wai), alongside the attractive inlet of **Three Fathoms Cove** (Kei Ling Ha Hoi) with its many fish farms. At **Sai Sha Road** turn right. ▶ The bus stop is 300 metres further.

The MacLehose option rejoins the main route here.

*Fish farms in Three Fathoms Cove*

# WALK 12
## *Ma On Shan Country Park*

| | |
|---|---|
| **Start** | Tai Shui Hang MTR station (Tuen Ma line) exit B 大水坑港鐵站 |
| **Alternative start** | Ma On Shan Country Park barbecue site 馬鞍山燒烤場 |
| **Finish** | Lake Side Garden bus stop, Hiram's Highway, Sai Kung 翠塘花園巴士站，西貢公路 |
| **Distance** | 9.5km (from alternative start: 6.75km) |
| **Total ascent** | 680m (from alternative start: 450m) |
| **Grade** | Moderate (from alternative start: easy; with optional summit: difficult) |
| **Time** | 4hr (from alternative start: 3hr) |
| **Terrain** | Begins on a cycle path, then a mixture of stone and concrete steps, road and pavement, plus dirt, stone and concrete paths |
| **Summits** | Pyramid Hill (536m); optional extra: Ma On Shan (702m) |
| **Map** | Sai Kung & Clear Water Bay |

The Ma On Shan Country Trail is an excellent hike through a wonderful country park, but it does not go to the summit of Ma On Shan. To add challenge, Walk 12 includes Pyramid Hill and an optional extra to the top of Hong Kong's tenth highest mountain, Ma On Shan (馬鞍山 Horse Saddle Hill) via MacLehose Trail's best ridge walk. The route also includes a superb viewpoint and some historical mining relics.

The alternative start misses the urban portion of this walk, thus starting in the heart of the country park.

## Public transport

**Alternative start:** From Ma On Shan MTR station (Tuen Ma line) exit B, walk S through Sunshine City Plaza to On Luk Street. Take green minibus NR84 (infrequent service, every 1hr 30min; see Appendix A). Note that the barbecue area is not the last stop.

**End:** Take bus 92 to Diamond Hill MTR station (Kwun Tong and Tuen Ma lines).

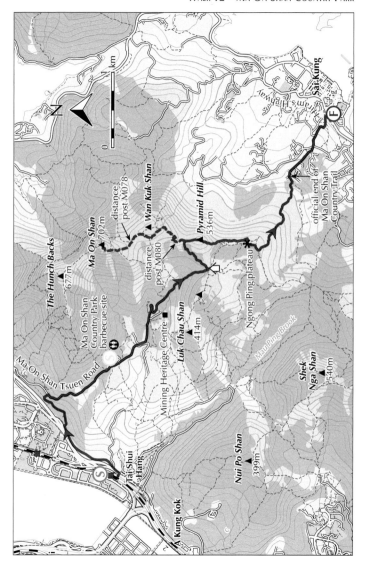

Sai Kung

Hiram's Highway

distance post M078

Wan Kuk Shan

Pyramid Hill
536m

Ma On Shan
702m

The Hunch Backs
677m

distance post M080

official end of Ma On Shan Country Trail

Ngong Ping plateau

Ma On Shan Country Park barbecue site

Luk Chau Shan
414m

Man Ping Brook

Mining Heritage Centre

Ma On Shan Tsuen Road

Shek Nga Shan
540m

Tai Shui Hang

Nui Po Shan
399m

A Kung Kok

N

0        1 km

From the MTR station, turn left (which is exit B), follow the tunnel to a T-junction, then go left (still underground) following signs for Tai Shui Hang Village. Once above ground, walk along a footpath next to a cycle lane for nearly 1km, go underneath a pedestrian bridge, then 250 metres later turn right along a concrete footpath. In about 500 metres by some mining relics, take a rough set of stairs on the right. ◄ This is along a small catchwater. The footpath almost immediately forks right, leading shortly to **Ma On Shan Tsuen Road**. Go right, uphill.

*If you miss this turning, simply reach Ma On Shan Tsuen Road and turn right, uphill.*

## MINING HERITAGE

There are occasional old mine shafts and relics along this route, the only evidence to suggest that this was once the largest mine in Hong Kong. Initially opencast then moving deep underground, the mine employed nearly 6000 people to dig out magnetite (iron ore). Some descendants of these miners still live in Ma On Shan Village, built to house the workforce. Ma On Shan Tsuen Road used to lead to the ore-loading pier, but since all the buildings and roads to the north are now on reclaimed land it no longer reaches the sea.

More information can be found at the Mining Heritage Centre located in Grace Youth Camp (admission free, open Fri/Sat/Sun and public holidays, 10am–5pm).

*There is a turning on the right in just under 1km, which leads in 300 metres to the Mining Heritage Centre.*

Walk up the road for 1km to **Ma On Shan Country Park barbecue site**; this is the alternative start point for this walk and the official start of Ma On Shan Country Trail. Continue along the road. ◄

About 1.5km from the barbecue site, the concrete road changes to a lovely path. Cross a stream and 800 metres later arrive at a **shelter**. Turn left, signed Kei Ling Ha, leaving Ma On Shan Country Trail and now following MacLehose Trail (in reverse). After about 500 metres, a narrow unsigned footpath goes upwards on the right, heading S. ◄ To continue with Walk 12, turn right onto this narrow path; alternatively, stay on the main trail for an optional ascent to the summit of Ma On Shan via a superb ridge walk.

*The footpath is about 50 metres before distance post M080, so if you reach the distance post you have gone too far.*

**Optional summit: Ma On Shan**
This adds 3.5km, 250m ascent and 1hr 30min. Where the narrow unsigned path turns off to the right, stay on the main trail and pass **distance post M080** after about 50 metres. Continue along MacLehose Trail (in reverse) for just over 1km via its best ridge walk to **distance post M078**. Turn left (not signed) and follow the path up, with some scrambling (although no danger), past some warning signs, and 500 metres later reach the summit of **Ma On Shan**.

*At the top of Ma On Shan*

Hong Kong is a highly safety-conscious place. Quite often there are warning signs, advising 'experienced walkers only' or 'beware of dehydration and heat exhaustion'. On the ascent to Ma On Shan is a sign saying: 'Danger: this path leads to an area where serious/fatal accidents have occurred. Please do not progress further.' It does not apply to the route taken by Walk 12, but rather to a rock-climbing area between Ma On Shan, The Hunch Backs and Tiu Sau Ngam, which is particularly risky in wet windy weather. It is a shame that the warning sign deters people from visiting the lovely summit of Ma On Shan.

Retrace your steps to **distance post M080**. About 50 metres later, rejoin Walk 12 by turning left (S) onto the narrow unsigned footpath where your Ma On Shan detour began.

**Main route**

*The Ngong Ping Viewing Point has awe-inspiring views, including Sharp Peak (Walk 13) and High Junk Peak (Walk 14).*

Ascend the narrow footpath (S) for 200 metres to the summit of **Pyramid Hill** (大金鐘 Big Golden Bell). On the other side, descend to **Ngong Ping plateau 昂坪**, which is famous for its views and as a take-off point for paragliders. ◄

Follow MacLehose Trail from the SW end of the plateau, then turn left after 200 metres, signed Tai Shui Tseng, leaving MacLehose Trail and rejoining Ma On Shan Country Trail. Continue along this beautiful path for 1km, reach a concrete path and follow it down for 300 metres to a road, the **official end of Ma On Shan Country Trail**.

*Top of Pyramid Hill, looking back at Ma On Shan*

Turn left (E) to walk through some villages along Pak Kong Au Road. At a crossroads 500 metres later, go straight ahead onto Tan Cheung Road, leading 200 metres later to a dead-end road called Sun King Terrace. Just 100 metres along, at the end of that road, take steps down, heading SE, and 250 metres further arrive at **Hiram's Highway**. The required bus stop is on the other side of the road to the left.

# WALK 13
*Ko Lau Wan to Sharp Peak*

| | |
|---|---|
| **Start** | Ko Lau Wan 高流灣 |
| **Finish** | Pak Tam Au 北潭凹 |
| **Distance** | 15.5km |
| **Total ascent** | 1080m |
| **Grade** | Challenging |
| **Time** | 7hr |
| **Terrain** | Begins with dirt paths, followed by the ascent and descent of Sharp Peak on difficult scree slopes with occasional scrambling; after a short beach section, the walk finishes with easy walking on concrete paths |
| **Summits** | Tung Lung Mei Che (208m), Tung Lung Tau Che (222m), unnamed summit (168m), Sharp Peak (468m), Mai Fan Teng (363m) |
| **Map** | Sai Kung & Clear Water Bay |

Ko Lau Wan is a remote village with no road access. The ferry journey is a treat on its own, with views of Plover Cove and the 76m-tall Goddess of Mercy statue at Tsz Shan Monastery, Pat Sin Leng mountain range (Wilson Trail, Section 9) to the north, and Ma On Shan (Walk 12) to the south. After a short ascent, the route goes along a ridge, giving the sensation of wide open space, with views of the sea and of the northern and western slopes of Sharp Peak.

Sharp Peak is one of Hong Kong's three famous 'pointy' peaks, the others being High Junk Peak (Walk 14) and Castle Peak in the western New Territories. Named because of its distinctive shape, once seen it is easily recognised. After approaching it from the north and west, the ascent to the summit is from the south and descent is via the east. In our view, this is the best route up and down this austere peak: it is the easiest and the safest, and encompasses all four sides. This route is not recommended in bad or wet weather because of the steep scree slopes.

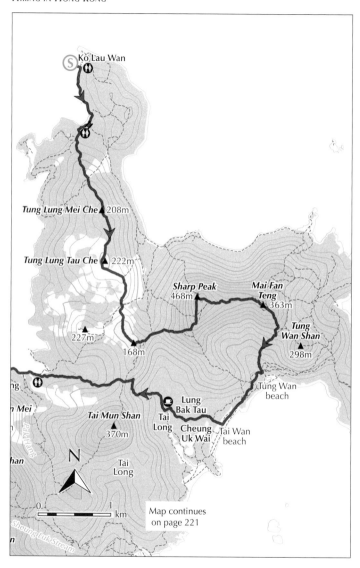

Map continues on page 221

**Public transport**

**Beginning:** From University MTR station (East Rail line) exit B, turn immediately left and follow the bicycle lane for 600 metres to its end. Turn left following signs for the pier, take the underpass, then go left for 400 metres to Ma Liu Shui Public Pier 馬尿水碼頭 for the *kaito* (街渡 small ferry). Important: from the underpass, do not turn right to Ma Liu Shui Pier 3. The ferry (direction Tap Mun 塔門) departs at 08.30am daily and the journey takes 90min; Ko Lau Wan is the fourth stop; see Appendix A.

**End:** Take bus 94 to Sai Kung bus terminus, then bus 92 to Choi Hung MTR station (Kwun Tong line).

Walk off the pier and turn right, signed Tan Ka Wan (meaning Boat People Bay). ▶ Arrive at some deserted houses after 750 metres, cross a **bridge**, and then 300 metres further, beneath some power cables, turn left from the concrete path onto an unsigned, unmaintained but well-walked small track.

Just over 1km later, arrive at the unmarked summit of **Tung Lung Mei Che** (東龍尾輋 East Dragon's Tail Mountain). Continue along this lovely, quiet ridge walk

The Tanka are a boat-living ethnic group from southern China. The people are now referred to as 'on-water people', since the name Tanka is considered derogatory.

A view ahead: the ridge to Mai Fan Teng, with Tung Wan Shan behind

This alarming notice refers to several serious incidents on the northern approach to Sharp Peak. It is very important to head east from the summit.

for 1.5km, past the unmarked ridgetops Tung Lung Yi Che (東龍二輋 East Dragon Second Peak) and **Tung Lung Tau Che** (東龍頭輋 East Dragon Head Peak) to a footpath crossroads, then go straight ahead (S).

Continue the ascent, admiring the wide and sprawling path to Sharp Peak summit on the left, go over another **unnamed summit** (no trig point) and 250 metres later curve left downhill. Go down to the saddle, where there is a strongly worded warning sign. ◄

Go up the steep gravelly path, which divides multiple times (all go to the summit, although the right-hand side is easier). After 1km reach the summit of Hong Kong's 60th highest hill, **Sharp Peak** (蚺蛇尖 Anaconda Python Pointy Tip). Go to the other side of the trig point, then fork right, heading E. The descent is long, difficult in places with loose scree, and goes up and over three little summits; the final one is **Mai Fan Teng** (米粉頂 Vermicelli Top, possibly describing the lines of loose scree). ◄

Paths skirt the tops but landslides make them less safe.

About 1.5km from Mai Fan Teng, at the saddle before the ridge's last peak (**Tung Wan Shan** 東灣山), turn right

(SW) down a wide path. Continue the difficult descent for another 700 metres and cross over a stream, then the going gets easier. Shortly after, arrive at a flat area, head NW, initially away from **Tung Wan beach** 東灣, and cross another stream. Follow the path as it curves uphill; there are multiple paths running parallel to the coast, but you can take whichever you prefer. Arrive 600 metres later at **Tai Wan beach**.

The name **Tai Wan** 大灣 means simply Big Bay, and the beach is a huge expanse of beautiful pristine sand. However, it is not safe to swim here because of rip tides.

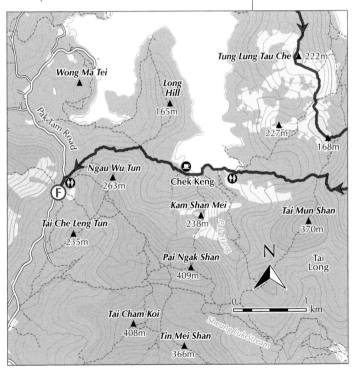

221

These remote villages were abandoned in the 1970s as it was difficult for residents to access work and schooling.

Halfway (about 300 metres) along the beach, just before a sign with a warning against swimming, turn right along a footpath. Follow this through the deserted villages of **Cheung Uk Wai** 張屋圍 at 400 metres along and **Lung Bak Tau** 龍鼻頭 300 metres later. ◄

At a T-junction with another path 300 metres later, turn left, then cross a stream to **Tai Long** village 大浪. Thereafter follow MacLehose Trail heading NW signed Chek Keng and Pak Tam Au, on a long unrelenting ascent through dense woodland. Then lose that altitude and arrive 2.5km later at the mangrove-lined water's edge, with a beautiful view of the bay.

About 500 metres further, walk through the decrepit and near deserted village of **Chek Keng** 赤徑 and fork right at its end. At a junction 1km later, follow the main path as it curves left, uphill (W). After 1.3km, reach **Pak Tam Road**, and the bus stop for Sai Kung is 100 metres to the left on this side (the east side) of the road.

## MANGROVES

A mangrove is any shrub or small tree that grows in coastal salty water, only found in the tropics. These highly adapted plants can cope not only with the salt but also with the wind and waves plus very low oxygen levels in the mud. The world needs more of these, as they stabilise coastlines, protect land from typhoons and rising sea levels, and according to NASA are one of the most efficient types of vegetation for removing carbon dioxide from the atmosphere.

# WALK 14
*High Junk Peak*

| | |
|---|---|
| **Start** | Hang Hau MTR station (Tseung Kwan O line) 坑口港鐵站 |
| **Finish** | Po Toi O village 布袋澳村 |
| **Distance** | 8.75km (family route: 8.75km) |
| **Total ascent** | 600m (family route: 420m) |
| **Grade** | Moderate (family route: easy) |
| **Time** | 3hr 30min (family route: 3hr) |
| **Terrain** | Begins with an urban section on pavement and quiet road, followed by good dirt tracks with some scrambling for the summits |
| **Summits** | Miu Tsai Tun (333m), High Junk Peak (344m); optional: Tin Ha Shan (273m) |
| **Map** | Sai Kung & Clear Water Bay |

High Junk Peak in Chinese is 釣魚翁 Tiu Yue Yung, meaning Old Fisherman's Peak, because its shape resembles a fisherman's traditional conical bamboo hat. Along with Sharp Peak (Walk 13) and Castle Peak in the western New Territories, High Junk Peak is one of Hong Kong's three famous 'pointy' peaks. Although it is not as distinctly shaped as Sharp Peak, being further south its summit gives a splendid panoramic view of Victoria Harbour, Hong Kong Island, Tung Lung Chau (Walk 18) and Clear Water Bay.

Beginning directly from the MTR station, this unofficial, unsigned but delightful route progresses quickly from the urban area to a country park. Families can avoid the steep slopes by walking on relatively level parallel routes, although the best views are from the short and sharp climbs. Bonuses include an ancient temple, a rock inscription and waterside seafood restaurants at the journey's end.

## Public transport

**End:** Take green minibus 16 to Po Lam MTR station (Tseung Kwan O line) 寶琳港鐵站.

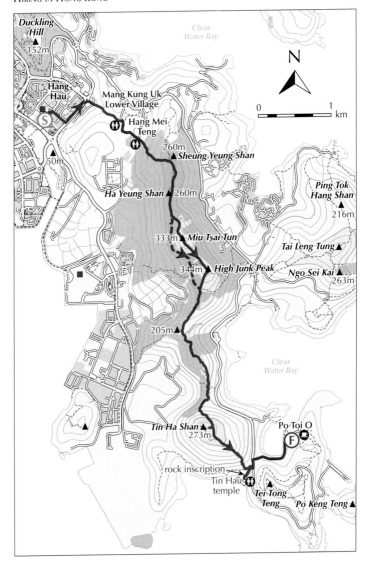

From the MTR station exit B1 on Pui Shing Road, turn left then immediately right down Ngan O Road. At its end, turn left using the subway, then walk next to a cycle track. At a roundabout 400 metres later, turn right along the short Po Ning Road, and at its end go straight ahead up a footpath, a beautiful green tunnel heading uphill along a valley serenaded by the river to the right.

Walk along for 500 metres, past **Mang Kung Uk Lower Village** 孟公屋下村 to a road. Turn right, go across a bridge and up along the road for 150 metres, signed O Pui village. At the T-junction, go left, uphill, for 200 metres to **Hang Mei Teng** 坑尾頂 and fork right at the **toilets**. When the road turns 90 degrees left after 100 metres, take the footpath going straight ahead. It then forks; take the leftmost (SE) one, a stone-lined path.

Follow this delightful 'old way' between villages for 200 metres then turn left up a rough steep dirt track, heading SE (ahead is blocked by a barrier). About 400 metres up, reach a footpath crossroads and take the main footpath going rightwards, downhill, signed Country Trail. Ignore paths off this, which are mainly mountain bike trails.

When the path forks 800 metres later, take the unsigned left fork. ▶ This leads in 400 metres to the summit of **Miu Tsai Tun** (廟仔墩 Small Temple Mound), where the reward is a view of an amazing number of islands dotted in a silver sea and the incredibly steep path ahead leading to the next peak.

Follow the short path down to the saddle then up to the next summit 600 metres further along, **High Junk Peak**. Continue along the same path for 20 metres, reach a popular photograph point with open views to the sea, then turn right down a rough steep path. At the bottom, 300 metres later, go straight ahead at the footpath crossroads, signed Tai Miu. The family route rejoins here.

Continue for 1.5km to a crossroads with a concrete path and go straight ahead (still signed Tai Miu). When the path levels out 750 metres later, there is a difficult-to-spot turning on the right for the optional summit of **Tin Ha Shan** 田下山. ▶ The main route continues for another 500 metres to a road; turn right. Just before the gate of

The right fork is the easier family route, signed Tai Miu. It rejoins at the next footpath crossroads.

This adds 0.3km, 25m ascent and 20min. Turn right onto the path and follow it to the summit trig point, then retrace your steps to the turning.

*Tai Miu*

the golf course there are two footpaths on the right, both leading to the **Tin Hau temple** in 300 metres: the leftmost path has access to a **toilet**, the other to the **rock inscription**, so you could go down one and return via the other.

Dating from the Song Dynasty (AD1266), this ancient temple is Hong Kong's oldest and largest **Tin Hau temple** (天后廟 Heavenly Queen Temple), also known as Tai Miu, meaning simply Big Temple. It is dedicated to the deity of all seafarers, Chinese Sea Goddess Tin Hau or Mazu, the deified version of the historical figure Lin Mo (AD960–987) who is credited with multiple miraculous sea rescues. Her annual celebration on the 23rd day of the third moon in the Chinese lunar calendar attracts 40,000–50,000 worshippers.

The **rock inscription** dates from AD1274, the oldest dated inscription in Hong Kong. It records a visit by an official from mainland China who was in charge of salt.

The minibus would also stop here, but the village has seafood restaurants and shops.

Once back at the road, go left (N) for 100 metres then take the first right along Po Toi O Chuen Road. ◄ Follow the road for 600 metres to **Po Toi O** village and minibus terminus.

# WALK 15
## *Chi Ma Wan Country Trail (extended version)*

| | |
|---|---|
| **Start/Finish** | Lo Uk Tsuen bus stop, Pui O 羅屋村巴士站, 貝澳 |
| **Distance** | 21.5km (short version: 16.25km) |
| **Total ascent** | 1250m (short version: 1030m) |
| **Grade** | Difficult (short version: moderate) |
| **Time** | 7hr 15min (short version: 6hr) |
| **Terrain** | A quiet road at beginning and end, mostly along dirt paths |
| **Summits** | Miu Tsai Tun (301m), Lo Yan Shan (303m) |
| **Map** | Lantau Island & Neighbouring Islands |

Chi Ma Wan (芝麻灣 Sesame Bay) Country Trail is Hong Kong's longest country trail. It is a quiet and easy-to-follow circular route with plenty of coastal views, a reservoir full of birds and interesting granitic rockscapes in Ha Keng. After the initial ascent, it mostly undulates in shade, making it suitable even for a hot summer day. The worthwhile summit of Miu Tsai Tun gives one of the best views of all the walks in this book.

The trail was substantially revised in 2021, so please note that some maps may not be up to date and there may be the occasional warning sign saying the route is still being constructed. This walk follows the official route, which is the Chi Ma Wan extended version, but for a less arduous walk a shortened version is also suggested.

### Public transport

**Beginning:** From Tung Chung MTR station (Tung Chung line) exit B, cross the courtyard to Tung Chung station bus terminus and take bus 3M. Alternatively, take the ferry from Central Pier 6 (Hong Kong Island) to Mui Wo (see Appendix A), then take bus 1, 2, 3M or 4.

From the bus stop, head E for less than 100 metres, then at Bui O Public School turn right along Chi Ma Wan Road, signed Mui Wo via Shap Long. Walk along

Toilets and Shap Long campsite are 150 metres to the left.

Allow extra time for the incredible views here, taking in all the peaks of Lantau Island and much more, most likely in glorious solitude.

*Splendid view from the summit of Miu Tsai Tun*

this quiet road for 500 metres. The road then follows a wide tidal river for 1km leading to the coast, with a view of the beautiful, long, sandy **Pui O beach** 貝澳海灘. Shortly thereafter, pass a **Tin Hau temple** (dedicated to the Chinese Sea Goddess Tin Hau: see Walk 14), then the road begins to climb gently. About 800 metres along, turn right, leading to the **official start of Chi Ma Wan Country Trail**. ◀

Go straight ahead and up the steps by a signboard, signed Lung Mei via Lo Yan Shan. Ascend for just over 1km through a beautiful forest of low trees to the summit of **Miu Tsai Tun** (廟仔墩 Small Temple Mound). ◀

Next, follow the trail down then up again a few times, arriving 900 metres later at **Lo Yan Shan** summit (老人山 Old Man Peak, with firewatch building and trig point). Continue along, now signed Lung Mei, and 200 metres later fork left, signed Shap Long Irrigation Reservoir. At a footpath crossroads 1km along, go straight ahead, leading to the valley floor. Cross a beautiful river via a bridge then shortly afterwards arrive at **Shap Long Irrigation Reservoir**.

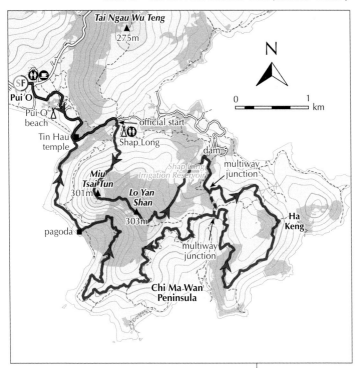

**Shap Long Irrigation Reservoir** was built in 1955 to supply water, not to Lantau Island but to Cheung Chau Island (Walk 16) via undersea pipes. Being so quiet, it is an excellent spot for birdwatching, with enormous numbers of three different types of egrets, plus black-crowned night heron and Chinese pond heron.

Follow the trail around the reservoir, turn right at the bottom of some steps (signed Lung Mei), then reach a **dam** and cross it. Thereafter go up to the top of some steps, reach a T-junction and turn right (same sign). After 150 metres, fork left uphill, signed Lung Mei and Chi Ma

*Little egret*

Short version: take the third option clockwise, signed Chi Ma Wan Country Trail, heading S uphill; rejoin the main route 400 metres later.

The short version rejoins the main route here.

Wan Country Trail. Arrive at a **multiway junction** with six options 250 metres later. To continue with the main, extended version of this walk, take the second option clockwise, signed Lung Mei via Ha Keng, heading SE. ◄

Continue along the quiet shaded path, enjoying good views of islands whenever a gap appears in the foliage. Arrive 1.5km later at **Ha Keng**, where there are fascinating rockscapes. Around 3.5km later, reach a concrete path and turn right, uphill, then shortly afterwards arrive at another **multiway junction**. ◄

Go up the steps (SE), signed Chi Ma Wan Country Trail and Pui O via Mong Tung Wan. Follow this easy-to-follow path as it undulates significantly for 5.5km. Towards the end, there are views of an impressive cliff of mostly bare rock to the right, which is **Miu Tsai Tun**, the first peak of this walk. Reach a crossroads and go straight ahead, downhill (same sign). After 400 metres, arrive at a concrete path next to a **pagoda** and turn right, signed Pui O. Reach the road 1.5km later and turn left, immediately passing the **Tin Hau temple** next to **Pui O beach**. Retrace your steps to the relevant Lo Uk Tsuen bus stop.

# WALK 16
## *Cheung Chau*

| | |
|---|---|
| **Start/Finish** | Cheung Chau Pier 長洲碼頭 |
| **Distance** | 12.5km |
| **Total ascent** | 470m |
| **Grade** | Moderate |
| **Time** | 4hr 30min |
| **Terrain** | A mixture of steps, and dirt, stone and concrete paths, road, beach and scrambling around a cave |
| **Map** | Lantau Island & Neighbouring Islands |

Not the usual summit-filled walk but a fantastic stroll around the relaxed, car-free island of Cheung Chau (長洲 Long Island), still an active fishing community. This walk is great for families, as children will love the pirate cave and enjoy trying to identify the many named stones of the Mini Great Wall. At journey's end, there is the opportunity to swim or sample incredibly fresh seafood.

## Public transport

**Beginning:** From Hong Kong MTR station (Tung Chung line) exit A, go to Central Pier 5 and take one of the frequent ferries to Cheung Chau (see Appendix A).

From the pier, turn left (N). At the end of the harbour go straight ahead and follow the main path past the fire station. ▸ Follow the main road (Cheung Kwai Road) along the coast; it becomes lovely and quiet as soon as it is out of the main town. Then, 1.8km from the pier, turn right onto **Cheung Pak Road**. Take the second path on the left 900 metres later, up a set of steps signed North Lookout Pavilion.

At the next junction, go left, following signs for Tung Wan Tsai. Take the next right-hand turn to go down the

The island has tiny fire engines, police cars and ambulances, necessary for these narrow winding streets.

The pavilion is the best place to see why Cheung Chau is nicknamed 'Dumbbell Island': it consists of two granitic masses joined by an isthmus.

The Tin Hau temple is dedicated to the Chinese Sea Goddess Tin Hau (see Walk 14), while Pak Tai Temple is in honour of the Taoist Sea God Pak Tai.

steps (beyond is a poorly maintained overgrown northward path) to **Tung Wan Tsai beach** (東灣仔 Little East Bay). Cross the beach and climb the very long set of steps at its other end to the **North Lookout Pavilion北眺亭**. ◄

Go straight ahead and walk down the stairs to the road, then cross it to the footpath signed Pak Tai Temple, heading W. Arrive at a T-junction by a group of shelters 750 metres later, turn left and immediately go left again, down steps. About 200 metres later, pass a small Tin Hau temple on the left, then arrive at **Pak Tai Temple 北帝廟**. ◄ Walk straight ahead between it and the basketball court along Pak She Street. Continue straight ahead for 150 metres to a crossroads with a shrine on the left and house no. 61 on the right, and turn left. Walk to the sea front and turn right along **Tung Wan beach 東灣海灘**.

Go along the coast for 100 metres to a second beach, **Kwun Yam beach 觀音海灘**. From here, follow the path inland and upwards, signed Mini Great Wall. About 100 metres later, go straight across a crossroads

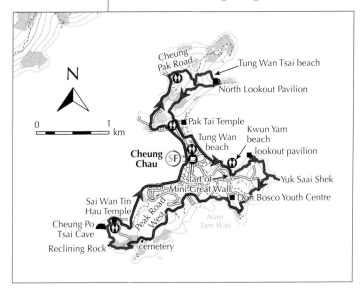

(left is Kwun Yam Temple, dedicated to the Goddess of Mercy), then immediately fork left to the **start of Mini Great Wall**.

> Named after the Great Wall of China and superbly built out of granite, the **Mini Great Wall** is a trail around 16 weathered stones, with names including Loaf Rock and Human Head Rock – though imagination is definitely required! Allow extra time for exploring; directions to individual rocks are not given below, but the paths are easy to find, with a mapboard at the beginning.

Follow the Mini Great Wall to the second shelter 400 metres along, where there is a worthwhile excursion. Take the first set of steps on the left, down to a **lookout pavilion** with views at sea level. Return to the shelter and take the other set of steps, on the left. Follow the Mini Great Wall to its end 1km later at **Yuk Saai Shek** (玉璽石 Emperor's Seal Rock). Retrace your steps for 150 metres, then take the steps upwards on the left, signed Fa Peng.

Continue on the main footpath for 300 metres, then turn left signed Nam Tam Wan. At the T-junction at the end, go right, downhill. Shortly after **Don Bosco Youth Centre**, reach a junction and go left (same sign). Walk past another Tin Hau temple at **Nam Tam Wan** bay 南氹灣, then go up some steps. Reach a road and turn left, then shortly afterwards go left again onto Cheung Chau Peak Road. At a shelter 400 metres later, fork left along **Peak Road West**. Just after the **cemetery** 1.2km later, go left along a footpath signed Pak Tso Wan. Reach a beach then follow the concrete footpath on the right signposted **Reclining Rock**, which is 400 metres along. ▶

The concrete path ends at some huge rocks; walk across them, then along the beach to where the path restarts. ▶ The path, now rather fun, goes through some narrow passageways between huge boulders for 300 metres to a concrete footpath. Go left, downhill, to **Cheung Po Tsai Cave** 張保仔洞.

The Chinese name 五行石 means Five Rows of Rocks, a far more accurate description than the English version.

At high tide, you will need to climb a ladder and clamber over rocks.

*Cheung Po Tsai Cave*

This really was a pirate cave, belonging to **Cheung Po Tsai** (Cheung Po the Kid). Press-ganged by pirates aged 15, he was later adopted by their leader. Subsequently, he became the lover of the leader's widow and took over the pirate fleet, allegedly commanding 600 ships and 50,000 men. Despite being beaten in a naval battle by the Portuguese, he was allowed to keep his treasure by agreeing to be the leader of the Chinese navy's anti-pirate unit.

Go through the cave (great fun but incredibly narrow, and some crawling may be necessary) and out the other side. This arrives back at the concrete path which led to the cave; now turn right, uphill. At the **toilets** 300 metres later, turn left down some steps following signs for **Sai Wan Tin Hau Temple** 西灣天后廟, which you reach in just over 100 metres. After the temple, follow the road along the coast for 2km back to the ferry pier.

# WALK 17
## *Violet Hill*

| | |
|---|---|
| **Start** | Wong Nai Chung Reservoir Park bus stop, Wong Nai Chung Gap Road 黃泥涌水塘公園巴士站, 黃泥涌峽道 |
| **Finish** | Tai Tam Reservoir Road bus stop, Wong Nai Chung Gap Road 大潭水塘道巴士站, 黃泥涌峽道 |
| **Distance** | 5.25km (extended version: 8.5km) |
| **Total ascent** | 400m (extended version: 680m) |
| **Grade** | Easy (extended version: moderate) |
| **Time** | 2hr 15min (extended version: 3hr 30min) |
| **Terrain** | All on well-made paths; a mixture of steps plus dirt, stone and concrete paths |
| **Summits** | Violet Hill (433m and 436m) |
| **Map** | Hong Kong Island & Neighbouring Islands |

Violet Hill, Tsz Lo Lan Shan in Chinese, is named after the violet, not that we have ever seen this flower growing here. It is such a delightful gem of a peak and so close to the centre of Hong Kong that Walk 17 provides two route options: the main route follows Tai Tam Country Trail, while the second is an extended version with the addition of Tsz Lo Lan Shan Path. Walking along the latter feels like being deep in nature, despite being in one of the most densely populated places in the world.

Violet Hill has three summits: the two versions of this walk visit one summit each, while the path leading to the third summit is overgrown and unusable. In summer, there are beautiful violet-coloured flowers here, although they are not actually violets; they are the rare and protected Hong Kong iris, *Iris speculatrix*.

## Public transport

**Beginning:** From Hong Kong MTR station (Tung Chung line) exit B1, take bus 6 from the bus terminus across the road to the right.

**End:** Take bus 6 or 66 to Central Exchange Square for Hong Kong MTR station.

Nature and skyscrapers in harmony

Look out for Wong Nai Chung Gap Trail signs along the route, giving information about Hong Kong's wartime history.

From the bus stop, take the first set of steps on the left just after the garage, then almost immediately turn left along the first footpath (before reaching a road). Go underneath a road bridge 100 metres along and reach the official start of Tai Tam Country Trail, marked by a signboard. Follow the path (ignoring any turnings) through what feels like dense subtropical woodland, although a concrete tower block is hidden just behind the greenery. ◄

   In about 1.3km (where there is a sign saying Mount Butler Road straight ahead), go right up a set of steps marked with a country trail sign. Walk over an artificial plateau (the top of **Jardine's Lookout Service Reservoir**) 150 metres later, and carry straight on to the steps at the end. At the top, 300 metres later, is a **World War 2 pillbox**; turn right to walk along a catchwater signed Tai Tam Country Trail.

At the end of the catchwater 500 metres later, go up the steps then straight ahead along a road. Go past World War 2 ammunition magazines, then reach **Tai Tam Reservoir Road**; turn right, then shortly afterwards cross the road carefully and go up the steps (S). ◄ Follow this up for 1km to a fork.

This is Wilson Trail but in the reverse direction.

### Extended version

At the fork, go left, signed Tsin Shui Wan Au. Arrive 150 metres later at the **433m summit of Violet Hill**, where there are great views of Dragon's Back (Hong Kong Trail, Section 8) plus the huge cluster of Tai Tam Reservoirs. Walk down a very long set of steps for 1.3km, then turn

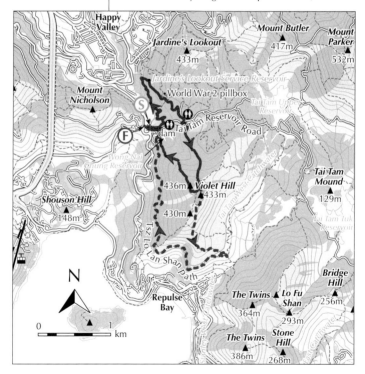

*The cluster of Tai Tam Reservoirs*

right, signed Wong Nai Chung Reservoir, leaving Wilson Trail. This is **Tsz Lo Lan Shan Path** (no sign).

Walk along this excellent track for nearly 2km, traversing the hill with some impressive cliff sections (safe with railings) and good views of Repulse Bay. The path then runs along a catchwater; after 1.7km, fork left onto a footpath signed **Wong Nai Chung Reservoir**. Almost immediately go up the first set of steps on the right, leading to the **dam**. Rejoin the main route here.

At the fork where the extended version leaves the main trail, go right, following signs for Wong Nai Chung Reservoir. The path dips a little then ascends, arriving 200 metres later at the **436m summit of Violet Hill** (紫羅蘭山). This is the nicest of the three summits, slightly higher and more open, with much better views. Descend along the path for 850 metres to a catchwater, turn left then immediately right, now following signs for **Wong Nai Chung Reservoir**. Very shortly afterwards, go up the first set of steps on the right, leading to the **dam**. ▶

*The extended version rejoins here.*

Cross the dam and arrive at **Tai Tam Reservoir Road**. Turn left, and at the end of the road 250 metres later is the junction with Wong Nai Chung Gap Road. Cross the road and arrive at Tai Tam Reservoir Road bus stop.

# WALK 18
*Tung Lung Chau*

| | |
|---|---|
| **Start/Finish** | Nam Tong Pier, Tung Lung Chau 南堂碼頭, 東龍洲 |
| **Distance** | 7.25km |
| **Total ascent** | 520m |
| **Grade** | Easy |
| **Time** | 3hr 30min |
| **Terrain** | A mixture of dirt and concrete paths with some steps; slight scrambling from the signal station to the campsite |
| **Summits** | Nam Tong Teng (232m), Sheung Kok Teng (86m) |
| **Map** | Hong Kong Island & Neighbouring Islands |

Tung Lung Chau (東龍洲 Eastern Dragon Island) forms the eastern boundary of the channel leading into Victoria Harbour. It is probably named after its 3000-year-old dragon rock carving, one of several rock carvings to be found around the coast of Hong Kong; measuring 180cm by 240cm, it is the largest in Hong Kong. Tung Lung Fort used to protect the sea route into the harbour until it was abandoned by the Qing Dynasty in 1810.

This is an exceptionally pleasant little walk, with wonderful views of the eastern entrance to Hong Kong and interesting coastal scenery as well as the rock carving and the fort, both of which are declared monuments of Hong Kong. Camping is permitted on the island, and there are even places to eat (open on ferry days only). The walk is suitable for children, especially if they find dragons fascinating.

## Public transport

**Beginning:** From Sai Wan Ho MTR station (Island line) exit A, turn right and walk NE along Tai On Street to Shau Kei Wan Typhoon Shelter Pier 筲箕灣避風塘碼頭 at the seafront; it is a set of steps with a ferry timetable poster, opposite the bus terminal. The ferry operates at weekends and public holidays only, eight sailings per day; see Appendix A. (Note that there are two ferry piers at Tung Lung Chau; get off at the first one.)

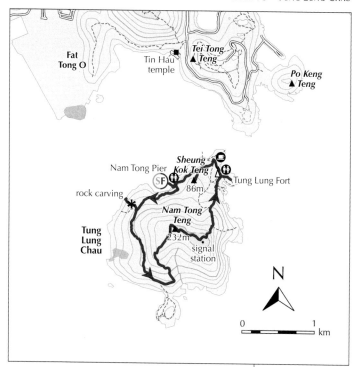

Walk off Nam Tong Pier and follow the path as it curves rightwards. Stay on the main path for 200 metres, ignoring multiple little turnings to houses, cafés and shops, then fork right following signs for Ancient Rock Carving. Continue for 200 metres to a T-junction, go right then almost immediately arrive at a **viewpoint**.

> There are marvellous vistas from the **viewpoint**: to the north, High Junk Peak and the largest and oldest Tin Hau temple in Hong Kong (Walk 14); and to the west, the final section of Hong Kong Trail, Dragon's Back, leading to Big Wave Bay.

Fantastic waves at the end of the fort promontory

This and other rock carvings around the coast are thought to be efforts by early inhabitants, perhaps fishermen, to placate the sea gods.

This huge edifice is a signal station sending radio signals to ships at sea.

Go down the steps for 200 metres to the **rock carving** 石刻. ◀ Retrace your steps to the T-junction before the viewpoint and take the other turning (S), signed Luk Keng Wan. Reach a junction 1.2km later and turn left, uphill (no sign, but the other direction is signed Luk Keng Wan). About 1.3km later, take a right-hand turn to the summit of **Nam Tong Teng** 南堂頂, then return to the route.

Continue for 400 metres, pass a helipad and arrive at a large round structure. ◀ The official small footpath is overgrown and impassable; instead, take an unofficial path following the fence line leftwards (clockwise) for 100 metres to a path heading NW. Despite being unofficial, it is well maintained, even with some stairs in places (minimal scrambling required). Go down it for 250 metres then fork left to head N.

Walk along this path for 800 metres, with fantastic views of two natural rock phenomena near the fort promontory: these are Spring Rock and Concealed Dragon Spitting Pearl, where waves crash into hidden caves firing white spume. There are multiple paths here, all leading to the **campsite**. From there, take a footpath on the right (E) signed **Tung Lung Fort**, which you reach 300 metres later. Go to the end of the promontory for great coastal views.

> The heavily fortified **Tung Lung Fort** 東龍古堡 was built in 1662 in the Qing Dynasty to guard against pirates, so that merchant junks could sail through the sheltered waters of Hong Kong to Guangzhou. It used to have 15 guardhouses and many cannons. But the island was too remote for replenishing provisions and maintenance, so it was deserted in 1810. The overgrown site was excavated in 1979 and declared a monument of Hong Kong.

Return to the **campsite**, then follow the concrete path from the **toilets**, heading NW for 250 metres to a café and shops (open ferry days only). Ignore signs for the new pier (Fat Tong Mun Public Pier). Continue along the path, following signs for Rock Carving. After about 300 metres, take a dirt track on the left, leading 200 metres later to the summit of **Sheung Kok Teng**. ▶

Return to the route and continue in the direction of the rock carving, arriving back at **Nam Tong Pier** after 400 metres. While waiting for the ferry, it is worth visiting Hung Shing Temple to the right of the pier.

Also called Hen Hill by the locals, it is not particularly high but does give good views of the eastern side of Kowloon Peninsula.

# WALK 19
*Mount Stenhouse, Lamma Island*

| | |
|---|---|
| **Start/Finish** | Sok Kwu Wan Pier, Lamma Island 索罟灣碼頭, 南丫島 |
| **Distance** | 9km |
| **Total ascent** | 620m |
| **Grade** | Challenging |
| **Time** | 4hr 30min |
| **Terrain** | Begins with concrete paths and steps, and the optional extra is via dirt path to a beach; access to and from the summit is on unmaintained, uneven, steep and difficult dirt paths through dense foliage with no signs |
| **Summits** | Mount Stenhouse (353m) |
| **Map** | Hong Kong Island & Neighbouring Islands |

This route is for the adventurous only, a wild and wonderful though difficult ascent and descent of the island's highest hill. Excellent navigation skills are required, and GPS and long trousers are highly recommended. If you want a break from going up and down the hard steps of Hong Kong, this is the antidote; but be warned – by the end of it you may be longing for those well-made stairs!

The route begins on easy paths on this delightfully quiet, car-free island, and includes deserted villages, beaches, and an optional extra to a turtle-nesting site. Both Walks 19 and 20 are on Lamma Island, so you could easily combine them for a long exploration.

## Public transport

**Beginning:** From Hong Kong MTR station (Tung Chung line) exit A, follow signs for Central Pier 4. The ferry journey is about 30min; ferries are every 1–2hr; see Appendix A. (Note that there are two ferry piers on Lamma Island; be sure to take the ferry going to Sok Kwu Wan.)

Walk off Sok Kwu Wan Pier and turn left (NE), going parallel to the coastline and following signs for Mo Tat.

At a junction 1.7km along, turn right along the main path, signed Tung O. Follow the path and walk through **Mo Tat New Village** 模達新村 then 200 metres later through the partially ruined **Mo Tat Old Village** 模塔老村.

> **The Chan and the Chou clans** have lived here for centuries. When Mo Tat Old Village was eaten by termites, most residents moved further north to the new village.

Walk past the disused rice paddies, now full of ginger lilies. ▷ Follow the main path for 1km, ignoring any turnings, to the ruins of **Old Yung Shue Ha Village**

The headily fragrant, waxy white flowers of the wild, invasive, non-edible ginger lily (*Hedychium coronarium*) flower from August to December.

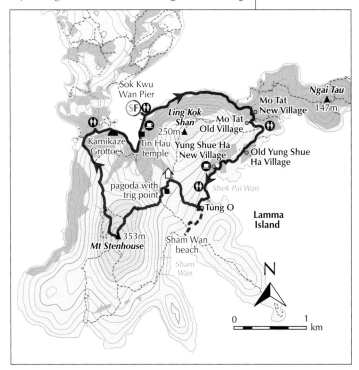

## LAMMA ISLAND

Lamma Island is the third biggest island in Hong Kong, inhabited since the Neolithic age. Chinese settlements started here in the 17th century.

Lamma Island acquired its name by mistake: the British misinterpreted the word *lama*, written near the island on a Portuguese navigation chart. This meant 'mud', referring to the silt at the mouth of Pearl River. The extra 'm' was a bonus when the word was inserted on the British charts! Coincidentally, it sounded like 'south fork' in Chinese, which describes the shape and the location of the island, being one of the southernmost islands of the Hong Kong territory.

*There is a café here with irregular opening hours.*

老榕樹下村. Continue along the path and walk through **Yung Shue Ha New Village** at **Shek Pai Wan** (石排灣 Rows of Rock Bay) 150 metres later. ◀

Then walk along a concrete path at the top of a lovely quiet beach. About 500 metres along, follow the path as it turns right, inland, through the nearly deserted **Tung O Village** 東澳村. Near the end of the village, 250 metres along, continue following the main path as it curves to the right, signed Sok Kwu Wan. There is an optional extra here.

*Sham Wan beach*

### Optional extra to Sham Wan beach

This adds 1.2km, 30m ascent and 20min. When the main path curves right in **Tung O Village**, take a left-hand turn and arrive at the beach at **Sham Wan** 深灣 600 metres later. Neolithic relics have been found here, and green turtles come to lay their eggs. (Note that there is no access to the beach during their breeding season, 1 June to 31 October.) Retrace your steps to the main route.

At the end of Tung O Village by some dilapidated houses, follow the path as it curves right and upwards. About 750 metres later, at a footpath crossroads with a **shelter**, turn left, signed Shan Tei Tong. Continue for 50 metres to a **pagoda with a trig point**.

The route now becomes a narrow rough dirt path, which immediately forks; go right (W). About 250 metres later, fork right, and the path is more overgrown. Go down for about 100 metres then begin to ascend, with some scrambling and a fixed rope in places. At a fork 200 metres later, go left, then 300 metres further fork left, downhill for a short time (ignore a right downhill turn after 100 metres). Towards the top, the path branches multiple times; take any of them to reach the summit of **Mount Stenhouse** 山地塘 about 300 metres later. ▶

There are two paths at the summit: take the right-hand turn (W), just before the trig point, after which the navigation gets more difficult and the path is not easy to follow. About 200 metres along, at a patch of bare rock, go right (N). Pushing through foliage (with difficult footing), continue heading downwards and N for 350 metres. Cross over a small stream then ascend for a short distance before the steep and uneven descent continues. About 300 metres further, at a fork by a huge boulder, go left. If you lose the path, aim for the top of the ridge that links the north and south portions of Lamma Island.

Arrive at a concrete path 750 metres later and follow it downhill. Continue for 250 metres, then turn right at a junction just after some **toilets**, heading SE signed Sok Kwu Wan. ▶

The Chinese name is Shan Tei Tong, meaning Hill Land Pond (despite the absence of water), whereas the English version is named after an Edinburgh suburb.

To join this hike with Walk 20, turn left here, signed Yung Shue Wan. (Total distance: 14.9km; ascent: 890m; grade: challenging; time: 6hr 30min.)

*A rope-assisted ascent*

About 250 metres along, turn left at the next junction and follow the path for 750 metres along the shoreline, passing the **Kamikaze Grottoes** 神風洞 (where the Japanese hid arms and ammunition during World War 2: see Walk 20). Cross a bridge and then turn left, signed Sok Kwu Wan. After 250 metres, pass a **Tin Hau temple** (dedicated to the Chinese Sea Goddess Tin Hau: see Walk 14), go past some restaurants and arrive back at **Sok Kwu Wan Pier**.

# WALK 20

*From pier to pier, Lamma Island*

| | |
|---|---|
| **Start** | Sok Kwu Wan Pier, Lamma Island 索罟灣碼頭, 南丫島 |
| **Finish** | Yung Shue Wan Pier, Lamma Island 榕樹灣碼頭, 南丫島 |
| **Distance** | 6.25km |
| **Total ascent** | 270m |
| **Grade** | Easy |
| **Time** | 2hr 15min |
| **Terrain** | A mixture of dirt and concrete paths |
| **Map** | Hong Kong Island & Neighbouring Islands |

This lovely easy walk on a quiet, car-free island is mostly on shaded, rough paths surrounded by birdsong, making it suitable for families. It crosses Hong Kong's third-largest island from east to west, arriving at one pier and leaving from the other. The walk visits two major settlements, Sok Kwu Wan and Yung Shue Wan, with an opportunity to explore World War 2 grottoes along the way.

The chosen direction is because the ferries from the end point are more frequent, making it easier for the return journey; there are many eateries at the beginning and end of the route. Both Walks 19 and 20 are on Lamma Island, so you could easily combine them for a long exploration.

## Public transport

**Beginning:** From Hong Kong MTR station (Tung Chung line) exit A, follow signs for Central Pier 4. The ferry journey is about 30min; ferries are every 1–2hr; see Appendix A. (Note that there are two ferry piers on Lamma Island; be sure to take the ferry going to Sok Kwu Wan.)

**End:** Take the ferry to Central Pier 4; there are 1–2 ferries per hour.

The early settlers were fishermen, and Sok Kwu in Chinese refers to the tightening and gathering of the fishing nets.

Walk off Sok Kwu Wan Pier and turn right (S). ◄ Go past a **Tin Hau temple** (dedicated to the Chinese Sea Goddess Tin Hau: see Walk 14) and 250 metres later take the first right-hand turn, signed Yung Shue Wan. About 400 metres later are the **Kamikaze Grottoes 神風洞**.

**Kamikaze**, literally meaning 'divine wind', refers to the typhoons that destroyed the Mongol fleets threatening Japan in 1274 and 1281. Towards the end of World War 2, the name was usurped by Japanese nationalist propagandists to promote suicidal attacks, with explosive-laden aircraft deliberately crashing into the enemy.

During their occupation of Lamma Island, the Japanese hid arms and ammunition in several huge granitic caves, planning to launch kamikaze speedboat attacks against Allied warships, but they surrendered before this occurred.

In more peaceful times, these caves are famous for the discovery of an amphibian, Romer's tree frog (*Philautus romeri*), which is endemic to Hong Kong.

This is where Walk 19 joins Walk 20.

Go left at a fork after 150 metres and go straight ahead at the next junction 250 metres later (ignore a left turn to the **toilets**). ◄ This shortly leads to **Lo So Shing Village 蘆鬚城村**. At the crossroads in the village, go straight ahead and follow the path as it curves left, signed Yung Shue Wan. Next to two benches about 700 metres later, go right at a fork, signed Luk Chau. About 600 metres along, pass **Lamma Youth Camp 南丫青年營** on the left, then immediately after a left-hand concrete road, turn left onto a dirt track signed Lo Tik Wan. Follow it (ignore any side tracks) to a fork and go right (the left heads towards the **power station**). Continue along the main path for 1.5km to a concrete road. ◄

Right leads to Lamma Wind Power Station 南丫風采發電站.

There is a single wind turbine at **Lamma Wind Power Station**, Hong Kong's first and only one. Although much is made of this foray into renewable electricity generation, the huge Lamma Power

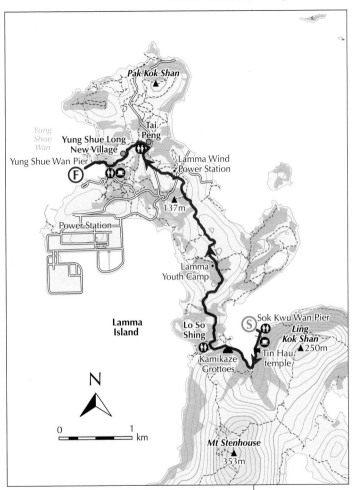

Station is exclusively coal- and gas-fired, and only 1 per cent of Hong Kong's electricity is renewable – a fraction of the 25 per cent imported from mainland Chinese nuclear power stations.

*Looking back at Sok Kwu Wan across the fish farms*

Cross directly over the concrete road onto a rough path. There are several minor routes: take any path, going uphill for about 200 metres to the top, then follow the main path heading NW for 250 metres to a concrete road. Turn right (downhill) then 350 metres later turn left, signed Tai Peng. Head NW for 100 metres then fork left just after some **toilets**. Go left at a T-junction after 100 metres in **Tai Peng** village 大坪村.

Follow the path for 500 metres through villages that merge imperceptibly with one another. In **Yung Shue Long New Village** 榕樹塱新村, veer right (not left to the old village), arriving 100 metres later at **Yung Shue Wan** (榕樹灣 Banyan Tree Bay). Turn right at the end of the path, and follow the main street through the busy town (many shops, restaurants and cafés) for 300 metres to **Yung Shue Wan Pier**.

# WALK 21
## *Po Toi Island*

| | |
|---|---|
| **Start/Finish** | Po Toi Island Pier 蒲台島碼頭 |
| **Distance** | 6.25km |
| **Total ascent** | 340m |
| **Grade** | Easy |
| **Time** | 2hr 30min |
| **Terrain** | Bare slabs of pink granite up to the summit, followed by concrete steps and paths |
| **Summits** | Ngau Wu Teng (188m) |
| **Map** | Hong Kong Island & Neighbouring Islands |

An easy short walk around a car-free island, with various points of interest. The first portion is especially enjoyable, walking on bare pink granite – the only such walk in Hong Kong. The terrain is mostly too exposed for trees, apart from around the sole village, giving the island an unusual landscape. At all times there are panoramic sea views, with waves crashing against rocks.

The island is famous for its peculiar-shaped rocks, edible seaweed and ancient rock carvings. There is also the chance to see interesting migratory birds in season.

### Public transport

**Beginning:** From Hong Kong MTR station (Tung Chung line) exit B1, turn left, then first right and second left to Connaught Road C bus stop, Connaught Road, Central (in front of Jardine House). Take bus 37B or 37X to Aberdeen Promenade, and catch the *kaito* (small ferry) from Tsui Wah floating pier 翠華浮橋碼頭 (along the promenade near Aberdeen Pier). The ferry operates on Tuesdays, Thursdays, weekends and public holidays, with once daily sailings; see Appendix A.

**End:** Take the *kaito* to Aberdeen Pier. Cross the road via the pedestrian bridge to Aberdeen bus stop, then take bus 70 to Central Exchange Square for Hong Kong MTR station.

## PO TOI ISLAND

Po Toi Island means Seaweed Island, and seaweed is still harvested and sold here. Known as the South Pole of Hong Kong, the island has been inhabited for more than 3500 years, although with no mains water or electricity it is now in decline. The school closed in the 1980s and many residents have moved to the city.

There are shops and restaurants selling seaweed around here.

Walk off the pier into **Wan Tsai**, the island's sole village, and turn left. ◄ Follow the path parallel to the shoreline for 800 metres to a T-junction. Go left to explore the Miu Kok **Tin Hau temple** 廟角天后廟 (one of many such temples

254

found around Hong Kong, dedicated to the Sea Goddess Tin Hau: see Walk 14) and Conch Rock, then return to the junction. Go up the other path on the right, following signs for Route 3 (Rugged Trail), then immediately fork left. ▶ Continue for 3km along what is more a suggested route rather than a proper path; this is an unusual and delightful section, walking across large slabs of the island's famous pink granite, marked by poles and the occasional direction indicator, and surrounded by low shrubs.

Arrive at a concrete path and turn left, signed 'pavilion' (right is back to the pier). Continue for about 500 metres to the summit of **Ngau Wu Teng** (牛湖頂 Cow Lake Top), followed 30 metres later by the pavilion. Take the long staircase down for 600 metres to a T-junction (with **toilet**), enjoying unobstructed views of the South China Sea and Ngong Chong Peninsula (the southern tip of this island).

Go left, signed Monk Rock (right goes back to the pier). About 300 metres along, arrive at Monk Rock 僧人石 and **Tortoise Rock** 烏龜石. ▶ Continue on the path, passing a **lighthouse** after 200 metres. About 150 metres later, take the steps heading down on the left to explore the fascinating rocky landscape, and continue to **Nam**

*A good display of fishing boats in the bay*

Beware of overhead cables around the town's communication shack.

Both Monk Rock and Tortoise Rock are popular photography locations.

255

*The Buddha's Palm*

**Kok Tsui** (南角咀 South Corner Mouth), the southernmost point of the island.

Retrace your steps to the main path, go left (N) and 150 metres further arrive at **Buddha's Palm Cliff** 佛手崖. Buddha's Palm Cliff honestly does resemble its name! After another 350 metres, arrive back at the previous T-junction (with **toilet**). Go left (NW) signed 'pier', and 500 metres along take the steps down on the left to the **rock carving** 石刻.

Apparently, there had long been rumours among local fishermen about the **rock carvings** on Po Toi Island, although they were not formally discovered until the 1960s. Now a protected monument, it is estimated that they were carved about 3500 years ago, facing the sea to propitiate the sea gods.

If you are too early for the return ferry, have a look at the Coffin Rock along Route 1, or try some local seaweed soup.

Retrace your steps to the main path, turn left and 400 metres later arrive back at **Wan Tsai**. Turn left at the T-junction, which leads to the **pier**. ◄

# APPENDIX A
*Useful contacts*

To call a Hong Kong number from outside Hong Kong, use the international access code for the country you're calling from (from the UK, the code is 00), then the Hong Kong country code (852) followed by the rest of the number.

## General information
For up-to-date information on travel to Hong Kong, see the 'Foreign Travel Advice' section on Hong Kong on the UK government website
www.gov.uk/foreign-travel-advice

Hong Kong Tourism Board
(has the links for all travel apps)
www.discoverhongkong.com

## Airlines
UK contact numbers:

British Airways
www.britishairways.com
tel 0344 493 0787

Cathay Pacific
www.cathaypacific.com
tel 0207 660 8992

Virgin Atlantic
www.virginatlantic.com
tel 0344 874 7747

## Transport
Transport in Hong Kong
www.td.gov.hk/en/
transport_in_hong_kong/
public_transport/

Online journey planner
www.hkemobility.gov.hk

Mass Transit Railway (MTR)
www.mtr.com.hk

Peak Tram
www.thepeak.com.hk/en
tel 2522 0922

Ngong Ping 360 (Cable Car)
www.np360.com.hk/en/cable-car
tel 3666 0606

## Bus
Kowloon and New Territories
(Kowloon Motor Bus)
www.kmb.hk/en
tel 2745 4466

Hong Kong Island
(New World First Bus and Citybus)
www.bravobus.com.hk/home
tel 2136 8888 (New World First Bus)
tel 2873 0818 (Citybus)

Lantau Island (New Lantao Bus)
www.nlb.com.hk
tel 2984 9848

Lantau Island North and airport only
(Long Win Bus)
www.lwb.hk/en/
tel 2261 2791

Minibus (green and red)
www.16seats.net/eng/

NR84 special minibus for Walk 12
www.wikiroutes.info/en/
hong-kong?routes=60632

### Ferry and *kaito* (small ferry)
*Kaito* (small ferry) for Walks 5, 6, 13, 18 and 21
www.td.gov.hk/en/transport_in hong_kong/public_transport/ferries/ kaito_services_map/service_details

Ferry services for Mui Wo (Lantau Trail and Walk 15) and Walks 16, 19 and 20
www.td.gov.hk/en/transport_in_ hong_kong/public_transport/ferries/ service_details

### Camping and accommodation
Agriculture, Fisheries and Conservation Department (for most campsites)
www.afcd.gov.hk

### Non-government facilities
Youth Hostel (Hong Kong YHA)
Bradbury Hall, Chek Keng
www.yha.org.hk/en/hostels/countryside-hostels
tel 2328 2458

Lady MacLehose Holiday Village
www.lcsd.gov.hk/en/camp/p_lmhv.php
tel 2792 6430

### Hiking
Enjoy Hiking
(Hong Kong government hiking website)
www.hiking.gov.hk

### Country park rules
Full rules for walking in the nature parks can be found on the Agriculture, Fisheries and Conservation Department website
www.afcd.gov.hk

### Maps
Survey and Mapping Office
(addresses and office hours)
www.landsd.gov.hk/en/about-us/sales-outlets.html
tel 2231 3187

### Visa
Hong Kong Immigration Department website
www.immd.gov.hk/eng/services/
tel 2824 6111

### Weather
Hong Kong Observatory
www.hko.gov.hk/en/
tel 2926 8200

### Other
Marine Life Centre (Walk 11)
www.wwf.org.hk/en/oceans/booking
tel 2526 1011

Hong Kong Museum of History
www.lcsd.gov.hk

Mai Po Nature Reserve
www.wwf.org.hk/en/wetlands/mai-po

### Emergencies
Contact the local police, ambulance service, fire department and other emergency services by calling 999. In Hong Kong, your call will be answered in Cantonese or English, since all emergency operators can speak both languages.

In an area covered solely by mainland China mobile networks, call 110. Your call will be answered in the official national language, Mandarin. The operator may speak English or may be able to find someone who speaks English, but this is not guaranteed.

# APPENDIX B
## Language and glossary

Cantonese is a tonal language with six tones: high, high rising, medium level, low falling, low rising and low level. A different tone is a different word, for example 'mm' said with a low rising tone means 'five', whereas 'mm' with a low level tone means 'not'. It is a difficult language to learn and speak, so we have provided a simplified pronunciation below. Note that, in the simplified pronunciation, a 'g' is always hard as in 'get', not like in 'gel'. Where a final consonant is indicated below by (), imagine getting the lips ready to say it but don't complete it, like the 'c' in French *blanc*, or the 'l' in 'owl'. If you are not understood, simply point at the relevant Chinese characters.

| English | Cantonese | Simplified pronunciation |
|---------|-----------|--------------------------|
| *Good morning* | 早晨 | *joe sun* |
| *Good afternoon* | 午安 | *mm on* |
| *Hi/Hello* | Hi | *hi* |
| *I'm sorry, I don't speak Chinese* | 對唔住我唔識講中文 | *doy mm jew, ngaw mm si(k) gon(g) jun(g) mun* |
| *How are you?* | 你好嗎? | *nay ho ma* |
| *Goodbye* | 再見 | *joy gin (or bye bye)* |
| *Do you speak English?* | 你識唔識講英文? | *nay si(k) mm si(k) gon(g) yin(g) mun* |
| *Which footpath goes to xxx?* | 邊條路去 xxx? | *bin tew loh hoy xxx* |
| *How far is it?* | 幾遠呀? | *gey yuen aah* |
| *Please, can you repeat once more* | 唔該, 再講一次 | *mm goy joy gon(g) yu(t) chee* |
| *Please, can you speak slowly* | 唔該, 講慢啲啦 | *mm goy gon(g) maan dee laa* |
| *I don't understand* | 我唔明白 | *ngaw mm min(g) baa(k)* |
| *excuse me or sorry* | 對唔住 | *doy mm jew* |
| *thank you or please* | 唔該 | *mm goy* |
| *yes/no* | 係/唔係 | *hai/mm hai* |
| *left/right* | 左/右 | *jaw/yow* |
| *I'm OK* | 我好好 | *ngaw ho ho* |
| *straight ahead* | 直行 | *je(k) haan(g)* |

| English | Cantonese | Simplified pronunciation |
|---|---|---|
| over there/here | 嗰度/呢度 | gore doe/nee doe |
| one | 一 | yu(t) |
| two | 二 | yee |
| three | 三 | saa(m) |
| four | 四 | say |
| five | 五 | mm |
| six | 六 | lu(k) |
| seven | 七 | chu(t) |
| eight | 八 | baa(t) |
| nine | 九 | gau |
| ten | 十 | su(p) |
| twenty | 二十 | yee su(p) |
| thirty-four | 三十四 | saa(m) su(p) say |
| one hundred | 一百 | yu(t) baa(k) |
| four hundred and fifty metres | 四百五十米 | say baa(k) mm su(p) my ee |
| three hours | 三個鐘頭 | saa(m) gore jun(g) tau |
| ten minutes | 十分鐘 | su(p) fun jun(g) |
| How much money? | 幾多錢? | gey door chee(n) |
| seventy Hong Kong dollars | 七十文 | chu(t) su(p) mun |
| too expensive | 太貴 | tai gwai |
| cheaper? | 平啲啦? | pen(g) dee laa |
| Where is xxx? | 邊度係 xxx? | bin doe hai xxx |
| bus stop | 巴士站 | baa see jaa(m) |
| minibus stop | 小巴站 | siu baa jaa(m) |
| MTR | 地鐵站 | day tee(t) jaa(m) |
| pier | 碼頭 | maa tao |
| taxi stand | 的士站 | di(k) see jaa(m) |
| campsite | 露營營地 | low yin(g) yin(g) day |

Full view of Hong Kong Harbour from The Peak (Trek 1)

# DOWNLOAD THE ROUTES IN GPX FORMAT

All the routes in this guide are available for download from:

### www.cicerone.co.uk/1051/GPX

as standard format GPX files. You should be able to load them into most online GPX systems and mobile devices, whether GPS or smartphone. You may need to convert the file into your preferred format using a conversion programme such as gpsvisualizer.com or one of the many other such websites and programmes.

When you follow this link, you will be asked for your email address and where you purchased the guidebook, and have the option to subscribe to the Cicerone e-newsletter.

### CICERONE
www.cicerone.co.uk

# CICERONE'S INTERNATIONAL GUIDES

**INTERNATIONAL CHALLENGES,
COLLECTIONS AND ACTIVITIES**
Europe's High Points

**AFRICA**
Kilimanjaro
Walks and Scrambles in the
  Moroccan Anti-Atlas
Walking in the Drakensberg

**ALPS CROSS-BORDER ROUTES**
100 Hut Walks in the Alps
Alpine Ski Mountaineering
  Vol 1 – Western Alps
  Vol 2 – Central and Eastern
  Alps
The Karnischer Hohenweg
The Tour of the Bernina
Trail Running – Chamonix and
  the Mont Blanc region
Trekking Chamonix to Zermatt
Trekking in the Alps
Trekking in the Silvretta and
  Ratikon Alps
Trekking Munich to Venice
Trekking the Tour of Mont Blanc
Walking in the Alps

**PYRENEES AND FRANCE/SPAIN
CROSS-BORDER ROUTES**
Shorter Treks in the Pyrenees
The GR10 Trail
The GR11 Trail
The Pyrenean Haute Route
The Pyrenees
Walks and Climbs in the
  Pyrenees

**AUSTRIA**
Innsbruck Mountain Adventures
Trekking in Austria's Hohe
  Tauern
Trekking in the Stubai Alps
Trekking in the Zillertal Alps
Walking in Austria
Walking in the Salzkammergut:
  the Austrian Lake District

**EASTERN EUROPE**
The Danube Cycleway Vol 2
The Elbe Cycle Route
The High Tatras
The Mountains of Romania

Walking in Bulgaria's National
  Parks
Walking in Hungary

**FRANCE, BELGIUM
AND LUXEMBOURG**
Camino de Santiago – Via
  Podiensis
Chamonix Mountain Adventures
Cycle Touring in France
Cycling London to Paris
Cycling the Canal de la Garonne
Cycling the Canal du Midi
Cycling the Route des
  Grandes Alpes
Mont Blanc Walks
Mountain Adventures in
  the Maurienne
Short Treks on Corsica
The GR5 Trail
The GR5 Trail – Benelux
  and Lorraine
The GR5 Trail – Vosges and Jura
The Grand Traverse of the
  Massif Central
The Moselle Cycle Route
The River Loire Cycle Route
Trekking in the Vanoise
Trekking the Cathar Way
Trekking the GR20 Corsica
Trekking the Robert Louis
  Stevenson Trail
Via Ferratas of the French Alps
Walking in Provence – East
Walking in Provence – West
Walking in the Ardennes
Walking in the Auvergne
Walking in the Brianconnais
Walking in the Dordogne
Walking in the Haute Savoie:
  North
Walking in the Haute Savoie:
  South
Walking on Corsica
Walking the Brittany Coast Path

**GERMANY**
Hiking and Cycling in the
  Black Forest
The Danube Cycleway Vol 1
The Rhine Cycle Route
The Westweg
Walking in the Bavarian Alps

**IRELAND**
The Wild Atlantic Way and
  Western Ireland
Walking the Wicklow Way

**ITALY**
Alta Via 1 – Trekking in
  the Dolomites
Alta Via 2 – Trekking in
  the Dolomites
Italy's Sibillini National Park
Shorter Walks in the Dolomites
Ski Touring and Snowshoeing in
  the Dolomites
The Way of St Francis
Trekking in the Apennines
Trekking the Giants' Trail: Alta
  Via 1 through the Italian
  Pennine Alps
Via Ferratas of the Italian
  Dolomites Vols 1&2
Walking and Trekking in the
  Gran Paradiso
Walking in Abruzzo
Walking in Italy's Cinque Terre
Walking in Italy's Stelvio
  National Park
Walking in Sicily
Walking in the Aosta Valley
Walking in the Dolomites
Walking in Tuscany
Walking in Umbria
Walking Lake Como and
  Maggiore
Walking Lake Garda and Iseo
Walking on the Amalfi Coast
Walking the Via Francigena
  Pilgrim Route – Parts 2&3
Walks and Treks in the
  Maritime Alps

**MEDITERRANEAN**
The High Mountains of Crete
Trekking in Greece
Walking and Trekking in Zagori
Walking and Trekking on Corfu
Walking in Cyprus
Walking on Malta
Walking on the Greek Islands –
  the Cyclades

For full information on all our guides, books and eBooks, visit our website:
**www.cicerone.co.uk**